MW01675035

I read the stories from Scott Stowell's new book *Back Road Grace* and felt at home instantly. I get it. Life up north is different from city life.

He mentions self-reliance, a word familiar to those who live almost-off-grid or completely off. Weather extremes, fire, thousands of wilderness lakes, and abundant wildlife shape a particular lifestyle. To survive, one must reinvent because there is no norm. Nature is the boss.

Yet, the wilderness speaks to everyone who visits Ely, Minnesota. Amazingly, many who visit return for good. Simple experiences can become monumental memories in the north woods. Scott reminds us how the little things are profoundly significant in defining the quiet pleasures deep inside each one of us. It's a fine read, tough to put down.

Layne Kennedy
Worldwide magazine assignment photographer
Author, *Beyond the Light: The Stories Behind The Photographs*
published, fall 2023

Back Road Grace

Scott Stowell

Share your stories.
Scott
Stowell

Ely, Minnesota
2024

For information, visit: writingoutfitter.com

ISBN: 979-8-218-36045-0

Selected references:
Bottom of the 33rd, 2011, Dan Barry
VH1 Storytellers, 1999, Tom Petty and the Heartbreakers;
interview excerpt, Tom Petty's Birthday Bash, 2020, Tom Petty
Herbal Rituals, 1998, Judith Berger
KAXE, March 23, 2018; IndieWire, May 25, 2018, Karl Jacob
Minnesota State High School Clay Target League, mnclaytarget.com
St. Louis County Sheriff's Department public records
Baseball: A Film by Ken Burns, 1994
A League of Their Own, 1992, Sony Pictures

First edition. Printed in Duluth, Minnesota, 2024

Photography and design by Scott Stowell

For Mom and Dad
who showed me ways to get from there to here.

For DyAnne
who has lived so much of the adventure with me.

Acknowledgements

To my friend Pace for helping me better understand
the scientific side of the natural world.

To Michael Goldberg and Heidi Holtan of KAXE/KBXE
Northern Community Radio for broadcasting
many of these stories.

This publication is made possible in part by:

a grant from Ely's Donald G. Gardner Humanities Trust

and an Individual Artist Project Grant made possible in part by
the voters of Minnesota through a grant from
the Arrowhead Regional Arts Council
thanks to a legislative appropriation from the Arts and Cultural
Heritage Fund.

Contents

Introduction

A misplaced chromosome lurked somewhere in my gene pool. It began in Philadelphia where I was born but wasn't supposed to remain. The chromosome worked me midway across the country, then elbowed me northward. My parents were not to blame. Actually, they were in cahoots with the chromosome to recalibrate this geographic oversight.

While my folks freely imparted guidance, they also knew when to let me discover my own inefficiencies. Mom's parenting was generally lower-key. Dad's more thunderous moments usually attracted my attention instantly. But he included me in his time whenever possible and seemed to like having me along.

The outdoors came first, mostly in the form of family camping and fishing. Hunting evolved later. But around the house, I raked leaves into a pile and played with fire while my folks monitored my match-striking technique to get the flames going. Eventually, I turned six. By then I could bait my own hook, whittle kindling into fire shavings and recommend which tent poles Dad was misusing to set up camp. It was the kind of growth that made my chromosome fidget.

By coincidence, my dad had found new employment and we moved to the Chicago suburbs. His improved tax bracket enabled him to purchase a tent camper that slept our family of four.

Having started life as a big-city boy, Chicago fell right in line. It, too, featured attributes like high-profile arts and major league sports. Little League was a must for me because Dad had played professional baseball. When he didn't agree with the coaching I received, he took over my training. It boosted my confidence.

But Chicago had something foreign to both of us—hockey. We learned it together. At the time, the city limits of our suburb were designated by the barbwire fence at the end of our backyard. A thousand acres of cropland and pasture were on the other side. We skated on a slough no deeper than a puddle and I puck-handled around frozen cow plop. My dad also asked the farmer for permission to hunt the cornrows and we'd walk the field in fall hoping to kick up pheasants.

During summers, our family camped at a variety of public campgrounds surrounding the suburbs. One of our favorites was a little-known, privately-owned tract of wooded farmland. A shallow river ran beside it. We'd set clay pigeons in the muddy bank for targets, climb up the bluff above the river on the opposite side, then pop the targets with my dad's muzzleloader. When time allowed, I'd leave camp for an afternoon to explore the river bottoms, all the while pretending to be Jeremiah Johnson. To this day, the fragrance of rotten eggs and sulfur instantly triggers pleasant memories of burnt black powder from a 45-caliber flintlock. So does the smell of fertilizer on farm fields.

Before each school year started, we'd also make a week-long junket to the north woods. But over time, public campgrounds began wearing thin with Mom and Dad. Outdoor life was being overrun with fellow campers who were packed more closely to us than our suburban neighbors. However, my folks still needed a regular nature fix. So they bought six wooded acres in central Wisconsin and built "The Cabin." My chromosome was on the move.

The Cabin opened physical and spiritual doors for me. It taught me that inanimate objects have a soul. I learned the value of being mesmerized by flames in a fireplace. It kindled my dreams of owning a pickup and living in a small town. I'd have been a forest ranger, except the scientific side of my brain put up a fight. I realized I much preferred the ambiguous human-behavior side that we sometimes found in the Wisconsin bar culture on Friday nights.

The Cabin wasn't far from a university town that captivated me whenever we'd visit, especially the sporting goods stores with cool outdoor stuff I felt I needed. The university also had a hockey team. Considering my plans after high school included a career in the National Hockey League, that's where I enrolled. The hockey didn't work out. As it shouldn't have. But little did I know, my future spouse had been residing there since her birth. Her name is DyAnne (pronounced "Diane"). You'll be reading it a lot.

Our connection was a roundabout path that took years to manifest without our knowledge. We've wondered if we'd ever unwittingly seen each other years prior to our first physical contact. Like me, Dy had a passion for both nature and the arts, particularly literature, and especially writing it.

After we got married, we lived in our college town for several years and worked in the area. But through an alignment of quirks, we later found ourselves unemployed at the same time. My chromosome was feeling nomadic again. It got me downsized from my job as a magazine editor. Dy had also been helping a woman edit her memoirs for publication. However, the woman died and the employment ended.

We embarked on the standard job-search but continually came up short. After months of dredging potential employers, grinding out applications and rarely obtaining interviews, we looked at each other and faced a simple truth—we can be unemployed anywhere.

We started packing.

Since before we knew each other, we were both enchanted by the Boreal North. So we headed where the population is distinctly more sparse. We had met just one person in the entire region. We had procured no employment. We jumped and hoped wings would appear.

Now we're embedded in the Minnesota north woods like a couple of ticks in moose hide. We found jobs…then another and another and so on. Livelihood here sometimes requires multiple gigs, though not always in a field for which we went to college or had been previously employed.

Up here, the wilderness dictates everything from the economy to spiritual enlightenment. The forest, lakes and rock are precisely the images in postcards and movies we'd seen as kids. Only now that we're year-round residents, the landscape and wildlife are real, not a backdrop from some Hollywood soundstage.

The climate is real, too. Winter dominates over half the year. Wildfires and straight-line winds take no prisoners. Summer is savored, blackflies be damned. Window fans typically suffice for home cooling.

Harsh realities of nature have wrenched our hearts. We've altered perspective on some environmental issues. Gravel roads awaken uncommon forms of etiquette. Wolves, moose and bears occasionally walk under our street lamps. Sled dogs serve actual purpose transporting people and winter camping gear. One look at their euphoria on a gangline is sure proof that they love their jobs.

But perhaps most engaging is our own species. One friend's former high school shop class processed venison right in the classroom. We've met people who regularly mend flesh wounds with Super Glue. Moreover, I'm continually impressed with how small-town folks look after each other. Commonalities override differences and their character exudes depth and humor.

It's not Utopia and it's been any thing but easy. However, had we not made that move, I think our souls might have shriveled.

Many of the stories in this collection have been previously published in print or broadcast on radio. They're about the lifestyle and perspectives I've experienced from living in two small towns on the edge of this northern wilderness. But a chapter of my earlier years has been included to connect some of the dots on my journey.

For what it's worth, the calendar date of our leap of faith was never consciously planned. But by chance, our relocation anniversary is February 29—Leap Year Day.

Acclimation

What's in a Name?

The town is the kind of place where people in the witness protection program go to live. It was exactly what my wife DyAnne and I needed at the time. Not to vanish from thugs and mobsters, but more to shelter ourselves where no one would follow.

Its name is Buyck, an unincorporated hamlet in northern Minnesota just a few miles southwest of Canada. Actually, if I trailed a deer there during hunting season, I could have accidentally crossed the international border…with a loaded gun. But it's not as if anyone would have noticed. The population is so small, it's countable at any given moment depending on how people made it through the weekend.

The name is spelled B-U-Y-C-K, but pronounced "bike," like the short form of bicycle. For panache, a children's bike was affixed to the top of each town sign at the two road entries. A handful of buildings are scattered across the two- or three-mile stretch between the signs. They comprise the basics: a café, machine shop, firehall, church and two bars. According to local lore, one of the bars was also a brothel way back when. Today, that establishment features a different amenity—a nine-hole golf course.

We rented a house trailer at the end of a gravel road. The trailer overlooked a wandering river from the middle of an old farm pasture. But sitting up high, it was exposed to extreme weather. Summer's heat cooked us like a sweatbox. Mosquitoes found a way inside and we wore bug spray to bed. The repellant kept them from sucking blood, but couldn't fend off the torturous, high-pitched whine of their invisible hovering beside our ears.

Eventually, we tracked down their secret portal—the uncovered chimney of the unused fireplace. Then we choked them off with a screen.

In winter, the front door froze open and the rear door froze shut. Clothesline secured us inside the open door. A hair dryer, or a propane torch during power outages, set us free out the closed door. Winter gales had an easy shot at us. To prevent our garbage can from blowing across the river, we bungeed it at the top to a vertical deck post. One morning following a night of utter cold with no precipitation, I noticed the bungee cord laying on the deck. It encircled the base of the tapered can, but had retained the can's shape from the top. The elastic had frozen solid without the aid of moisture and was unable to contract.

However, our winter endurance paid big dividends during spring breakup when the river loosened its banks and huge ice floes broke free. We hustled down to the shoreline and spent an afternoon like the event was Macy's Parade. We gawked and pointed at mammoth ice chunks floating by in slow procession. Many were longer than semitrucks, yet they somehow negotiated sharp river bends without breaking in half.

The trailer kept us dry and warm enough, but running water could be a little iffy. We shared the water pump with our nearest neighbor. It was in his cabin. He was friendly and generous, but not much for explanations. After the first time the shower trickled dry, we determined he must have shut off the pump without telling us. For a while, our request for future water pump heads-ups appeared to go unheeded. However, we learned that he just had a different way of serving notice.

Clues went back to our first weekend in the trailer when he brought us homemade eclairs as a neighborly gesture. Later that day, we tried to take a nap, only to be jolted upright by gunfire directly outside the bedroom window. Our neighbor was sighting in his rifle for deer season from the picnic table between the houses. Recollecting this, we deduced that whenever he stopped by with eclairs, we could expect a water outage or other disruption that afternoon.

The people of Buyck possessed a self-reliance like none other. It was a community of loggers and contractors. If a leaf spring broke on a trailer, they didn't wait around for parts to arrive in the mail; they made it themselves. When a massive blowdown flattened the federal wilderness at Buyck's doorstep, the loggers happily and sensibly offered to clear out the downed trees. They asserted that everyone would benefit; they'd earn income while removing fuel that kindles wildfires. But red-tape bureaucracy doused the idea.

Buyck also afforded magnificent wildlife encounters. An entertaining, long-tailed weasel often showed up from under the trailer and perched right on the deck. A snappy dresser, his annual fashion statement transformed from a brown coat in summer to a white so resplendent in winter that he glinted iridescent green.

The term "self-reliance" can sometimes be misleading. Self-reliance is actually a collaborative effort with unseen forces whereby reality overrides intention.

By winter, raccoons had taken shelter under the trailer. Word had it that they'd do more damage than bears if they chewed their way indoors. So the landlord had a leg-hold trap set beneath the trailer. A week or more later, not a raccoon was in sight. But I glanced behind the trailer's side skirt and came upon the white weasel. He had taken the raccoons' place. He laid still and silent between metal jaws, the sheen of his coat as cold as snow. The trap kept raccoons from raiding our pantry, but at a heart-wrenching cost.

As names go, "Buyck," B-U-Y-C-K, is just a label for a road sign. But it doesn't represent all that resides there. When we look back on that place in our lives, we remember the backbone, tolerance and never-ending cycle of reality.

Fish & Visitors

Benjamin Franklin once said, "Fish and visitors stink after three days." But I'm guessing he's never been to Ely, Minnesota. Ely's economy thrives on inviting visitors to fish here for days on end.

In many tourist towns, the early season percolates with excitement. But depending on the town, Franklin's quote becomes gospel as days wear on and the atmosphere turns ripe. I know of a popular destination one state over whose food and beverage servers practice an annual tradition. On Labor Day Sunday, they hurl God-awful insults at leftover patrons to chase them off for the season. In that sense, tourists can be likened to wolves: They get blamed for whatever goes wrong even if it isn't their fault. If Wall Street crashed, wolves and tourists would take the heat.

We moved from Buyck to Ely and live here year-round. As a result, I've experienced tourism from both sides of the counter. I've served beer and cocktails to our guests, and I continue to shuttle paddlers to wilderness entry points because the stories they tell are so rich. I think it's made me a better tourist whenever I visit other places. For the most part, though, the place where I live is also where I want to vacation.

Let me get this out of the way. I won't pretend that the summertime congestion can't get to me. By late-August, cramped grocery stores and snug parking spaces test my temper. And face it, there are the few snobs whose sense of entitlement exceeds their sense of civility. I find outlandish driving far more interesting.

I've trained myself to never flip-off shoddy drivers primarily because I might know them personally. U-turns at the stoplight seem to be a popular adjustment for nonresident motorists who have lost direction. Traffic freezes like frightened rabbits in brush until the ensuing roundabout finds closure. But I've also watched a local acquaintance one-up that maneuver. He spun his car in the opposite direction, jumped the curb, drove down the sidewalk behind parked cars and reentered traffic between two trucks idling at the stoplight. Pedestrians waited for the light to turn green before emerging from cover.

Similarly, boat landings can incite random acts of rudeness. The angler with out-of-state license plates who parked their truck and trailer in the shoreline turnaround was rather irksome.

However, I've also come across locals who use boat landings as a beach. They commandeer parking spots with small sedans in areas designated for boat rigs. Then they clog the water access with bodies, coolers and inflatable toys. Backing a boat trailer through a sea of beach bums is a tight fit. Spotting snorkelers oblivious to the powerboats above water is downright dangerous.

Overall, though, I'm inclined to believe that most civil transgressions aren't intentional. They're just oversight or lack of awareness.

Several years ago, a couple sat down at the bar I was tending after the lunch rush. We were the only ones in the place, so we had time to share stories. They worked in a metro area and their vacation to the wilderness was a bucket-list junket. They were intelligent, had good senses of humor and were highly complimentary. "It's so beautiful here, I can't even look," the woman said.

Both acknowledged they'd love to live here year-round, but questioned what they'd do for employment. When she found I was formerly a magazine editor, she asked how I felt having been an editor and now I was a…then she cut herself off.

I knew what she meant and wasn't offended. I reminded her of where I get to live, then I added I'm not the only one who feels this way. Many residents have degrees, even advanced degrees, in fields completely unrelated to their employment here. An attorney is an outfitter. A chemist heads outdoor education programs. Self-employment is an option. The lifestyle isn't for everybody. Some people need multiple jobs to survive. But living here is more than a backdrop—it breathes life.

I don't know if we ever met again or of any decisions they made. But we wished each other well when we parted.

Like folks from anywhere, the travelers I've met take pride in swapping stories from their home turf and what they're about. Riding together in a wilderness shuttle gives us time to learn from each other. We compare climate, outdoor recreation, wildlife, wildlife regulations and wildlife recipes.

While the wolves, bears and moose up here might be scary to some visitors, they tend not to kill people. But I've discovered that those north woods icons have nothing on the gators, snakes and spiders in southern states. A shuttle passenger from Oklahoma told of a water moccasin who chased him down in waist-deep water. He managed to club it with a tree branch before its fangs hit paydirt. From this, I learned two things: water moccasins are aggressive; and if I'm ever in that predicament, I'll never outswim them.

For one woman embarking on a solo canoe trip, moose-enchantment seized her attention. As our shuttle and conversation trundled along the gravel artery to her entry point, I mentioned we were approaching a logging road where I had seen moose droppings a month before. Such was her rapture at the chance to experience real moose poop, she happily delayed the remaining drive. We located the droppings and she took a picture of them with her phone, placing her thumb directly beside one to give it scale.

Sometimes wilderness visitors with the least experience embody the most sincerity. A member of a group I transported discovered a tick on himself. The group discussed it and he said he'd take it home for a friend to see. I began thinking that maybe none of them had camped or fished before. Then another group member confirmed my suspicions. He was intent on the proper care for the leeches in the plastic locker. But it wasn't to ensure the leeches survived as fresh bait. He was asking about their survival period, what they should eat and how much water they would need.

I just can't find fault with such concern for other beings.

The more we learn about the wilderness, the more we learn about each other, the more we'll respect all of it. Call them what you will: visitors, travelers, sightseers, strangers or something less complimentary. Welcome, you tourists. Glad to have you.

North Woods Memorial

The crying ended and the celebration began. Church was rough.

This was the opposite.

The banquet hall beside the lake spoke to 100 years of weddings, graduations, and hook-n-bullet fundraisers. It was a spacious log structure built to take a licking. Ancient moose antlers adorned the doorsill above the entryway. Framed textile images of boreal landscapes charmed the walls. Box fans whirred in every other window to cool the place down.

A photo display of the honoree stood on a folding table beside the front side door. A reflection of Halloween costumes, summer vacations and deer seasons documented rites of passage throughout the years. The siblings gathered for a group picture to update the family history once more. The smart-ass brother-in-law was in charge of the shutter button.

Outside, Grandpas gave the hexagonal merry-go-round a shove as grandkids rode the spinning benches, painting the air with root beer belches. The aroma of Polish sausage steaming in the Nesco wafted to them through kitchen windows, a tantalizing reminder of the ham, roast beef and turkey cold-cut buffet to come. Stacks of pepper jack, cheddar and Swiss awaited Kaiser roll companions with dill pickle spears for the side. The chubby cousin twice removed hovered nearby, eyeing up the foil barbecue roaster and potato salad.

Casual attire fashioned the moment. Sport coats were a touch dressy and style leaned toward the uncle in a T-shirt. The words over his cauldron-shaped belly read, "What would Gretzsky do?" His vivacious niece in the summer dress who he hadn't seen since she was a seedling, yanked him onto the dance floor for a dose of three-step. Her lanky legs were now longer than his and she could see over his bald spot. Even people with no sense of rhythm stepped out in spirited fervor.

The band wiped sweat from their brows and dusted the dance floor with emotion for family and friends. They played everything from polkas to Tom Petty covers. "Mary Jane's Last Dance"—on accordion—isn't a tune the average person can easily un-hear.

This wasn't average to begin with. It was elegance. Pure and simple. An expensive affair in an extravagant locale would have been holiness at a discount compared to the richness that resides in the familiarity of everyday life, people and memories.

Shedding Winter

The entire liquor store emptied into the parking lot, staff included—a sure sign of the coming spring. It ranks with the first sightings of robins, float planes and Harley-Davidsons.

The group gathered around the back of a pickup and its owner flopped down the tailgate to display the fruits of his labor. He'd been hunting for antler sheds earlier in the day and came home with a bounty of single antlers that made their annual drop to the forest floor from the deer or moose who wore them. His cargo was a mix of both. One in particular was a sweet moose specimen, a well-preserved, root-beer brown shovel with a big palm.

In situations like these, human nature can't resist asking the big question, "So where'd you find them?" The guy simply smiled and shook his head. There was no use prying for geographic whereabouts. That'd be like giving up a favorite fishing hole in summer or a hunting stand in fall.

The sheds signified we'd reached that hopeful point in winter when enough snow has melted in the woods to uncover its treasures beneath. As sheds go, hunters are well-advised not to dawdle; they're not the only interested parties. Plenty of woodland critters are just as sick of winter as the next mammal and they want dibs on those bones for springtime nutrition. Antler sheds are full of minerals like calcium, phosphorus and protein, among others. They're real lip-smackers for squirrels, mice, fox, coyotes, bears, beavers, otters and other varmints. Between them, they'll likely have gobbled every antler in the forest by summer. So get to those sheds before gnaw marks show up.

Shed hunting is one of several cabin fever remedies. But each year, a few people push seasonal transitions beyond reason. Theirs is a malady without the cure of shed hunting.

For some anglers, the first sight of open water along lake edges triggers them to dig their boat out of storage. Never mind that the air temperature might be below freezing when the water isn't. They haul their boat to the landing and prep it for launch.

Amidst this lake-hopping frenzy, they sometimes mistakenly unlatch the winch hook at the bow of the boat before backing it to the water. That hook normally secures the boat to the trailer. Bunk-style trailers, those with carpeted slats under the boat to support the hull, are susceptible to ice-up in freezing temperatures. Unfortunate have been the overeager anglers who backed up with an unlatched hook only to watch their boat slide off the icy bunks, not make the water and crash to the gravel.

Other seasonal transitions are required by law and can get pretty spendy if people don't plan ahead. Fish houses for ice anglers up here must be removed from lakes by designated dates in March. The more permanent houses on wheels or skids that sit on a lake all winter will settle into the snow and ice surrounding them. Especially during periods of freeze-thaw, some houses submerge deeply, often into thick slush, and become one with the ice. Un-entrenching them can fall slightly short of employing acetylene torches and dynamite.

One frustrated fish house owner decided to literally cut his losses. His house was a homemade wooden structure. After a couple of unsuccessful hours attempting removal, he fired up his chainsaw, cut around the shelter's base, took off the upper section, then burned what remained on the ice.

Conservation officers are trained to take a dim view of such methods. The fish house owner was cited for burning prohibited materials that would eventually sink into the lake.

If winter has your favorite seasonal elixirs in short supply, try shed hunting. In the meantime, may robins and Harleys grace your spring.

Back Road Grace

A few gravel roads in the Minnesota Arrowhead end at the edge of the wilderness. Motorized travel simply stops. Magical places worth savoring appear. And the journey to them is an education in back road grace.

One of the roads I use often is a former railroad line from the logging heyday. It's not much wider than a single lane to begin with, but it narrows even more in some parts. A grandmother pine shoulders one side and a greenstone boulder bottlenecks the thoroughfare on the other. Add some snowbank to it and the road pinches together like a clogged artery.

Road rage doesn't cut it on a thoroughfare like that because it's infused with smell-the-roses transport. In summer, if a vehicle from behind appears to be in a rush, the tortoise in front pulls over to let the jackrabbit pass.

In winter, that's not always possible. Vehicles inevitably meet coming from opposite directions and one or the other voluntarily backs up, finds a wider spot and the other eases by. I've offered and accepted my share of give-and-take many times. And with that comes abundance. The final day of last deer season is one example.

Blaze orange clothing is highly visible through oncoming windshields and is a pretty good indicator of who's been in the woods looking for deer. I could tell that the driver in a truck coming toward me was feeling chatty because his driver-side window started going down when we got close to each other. By the time we stopped, the snowbanks had cozied-up our fenders and we could have reached out to adjust each other's mirrors.

The guy inside the truck tilted his hat back then pulled the brim firmly down—a most certain invitation for a story. I told him I'd seen tracks but no deer attached to them. If nothing else, I knew where they were when I wasn't around. He said he'd seen deer in his yard after dark. At least his motion-sensor floodlight helped remind him of what they look like.

He segued impressively to another story about a hunter in his group who slept in that morning and was late getting into the woods. My storytelling buddy said he watched from his deer stand as this sluggard practically ran uphill trying to overtake daytime. But about halfway up, the guy ran out of gas. He stopped, sucked wind like a turbine, then leaned on the trunk of a dead birch. Moments later, the birch pushed over, crashed to the ground and spooked every deer in the forest.

An approaching truck slowed as it came up behind our conversation. At the same time, I realized another truck was also closing in on my rear bumper. Both stopped and waited patiently. So my new friend and I wished each other good hunting, shifted into gear and kept the line moving.

I rolled forward about two car lengths. The next driver-side window went down. I jockeyed up beside the hunter inside. But in my side mirror, I also caught the scene at my back. Two trucks were stopped. Two hat brims faced each other through their open windows. Both brims nodded with stories.

Portkeys North

Trail of Intentions

My dad appointed himself recreation director for a family camping trip when I was too young to understand what "laugh about it later" meant. At the time, I'm not sure Dad understood it either, but he was determined to show us the outdoor life. The guy took a beating on my behalf.

It began with marshmallow practice after our first breakfast. We'd be having s'mores throughout the week and he coached my sister and me on how to toast the perfect marshmallow. Prior to that, my experience with a marshmallow skewer had been self-taught. I'd stick it directly into the campfire flames, heat the forks until glowing, then use it to burn the names of family and friends into a wooden plank or split log. Our German shorthair, Bruno, had his personal marquee prominently displayed above his doghouse door.

If life is about choices, then to this day my sister and I still question what Dad was thinking when he removed a flaming marshmallow from the fire. He studied it, waiting for perfection to radiate before blowing out the blue aura encasing it. Then, like the fire-eater at a circus, he placed the charred delicacy into his mouth. A lot happened quickly in the moments that followed.

The marshmallow came out faster than it went in. Dad took one step and flung the skewer toward the woods. It spun so fast in the air that it made whirlybird sounds across the sky. Bruno watched it sail overhead until it disappeared somewhere beyond the horizon.

Now this was outdoor fun my sister and I could get behind. It was hilarity beyond measure and became increasingly contagious with each snort and gulp we uttered.

But then our dad turned and faced us. From his lip to his chin, the marshmallow forks left two scorch marks that looked like snake fangs on his skin.

Later that morning, the image of this indignity had to be as fresh in his mind as the ointment on his chin. But God bless his persistence, he took me fishing anyway. He normally had several tackle boxes to house his collection of museum-quality lures. But for this trip, only two fishing rods and his special "traveler" box came with us, the one with hand-selected lures just for the occasion.

We'd been on the water a couple of hours without catching a thing before he said we should head in for lunch. But just then, I was poised to zing one of his Dardevle spoons toward the shoreline. I asked if I could make one more cast. He told me I had the stuff of a hardcore angler.

I let it fly and we watched the lure arc gracefully skyward…but never come down. It soared above an overhanging tree branch, draped across it, then wrapped around multiple times with ever-increasing speed. It dangled high above our heads, unreachable by outstretched arms or an oar. Dad cut my line, a favorite lure now an artifact in the landscape.

At lunch, the announcement of my mishap superseded us being skunked and anything remotely associated with hardcore angling. After we ate, Dad went off by himself and rummaged through his tackle. He returned with bobbers and a Styrofoam bucket, then asked if I'd accompany him to the bait shop. This tactical maneuver was designed to improve our luck. We'd use simple hooks, several dozen minnows and go out after dark to catch those fish by surprise.

On that night, a Coleman lantern illuminated our boat from the middle seat. Dad shut off the motor, then surprised me by handing over his fishing rod with the open-faced reel. Until then, my only experience was with a push-button reel that looked like a soup can. He explained I'd need to learn open-faced reels gradually. We were just bobber fishing and it didn't require much casting.

Shortly into our foray, I noticed a loop in the line on my reel. To fix it, I figured I'd spool out line until I reached the loop. But it was buried deeper than I realized. In the glow of the lantern,

I peeled off line by the yard until I finally noticed the softball-size bird's nest I'd created. About then, Dad turned toward me and asked how I was doing.

Blurts and sighs from behind tangled line made clear the mess we were in. We were down to one useable fishing reel. So we headed back to camp.

I'd have done anything to absolve my string of ineptitude. Having reached the landing, I hurdled the boat bow and splashed into ankle-deep water. I snatched the minnow bucket, the lit lantern and set them on the sand. I scurried back to the boat and yanked it completely onto shore.

Had I been looking, I'd have seen Dad leaning over the motor raising the propeller from the water. But instead, my helpful tug spun him over the motor and into the murky depths below. He emerged, drenched but unhurt, and slogged toward land.

I didn't wait around. The minnows and I fled up the log steps embedded into the hillside trail. Suddenly, my wet sneakers spun out and I splayed across the path. Minnows dumped into the woods. I scooped some up, then tried again to outpace the beet-red demon stalking me from behind with a lantern and the fangs of a serpent.

Bedtime mercifully arrived without further roil. But later, I woke and saw Dad standing at the camper entrance shining a flashlight through the open tent flap. Soon, everyone got up to look. Outside, a raccoon had removed the bait bucket lid and was feasting on remaining minnows. It looked around casually as if searching for tartar sauce. Dad told us to stay put. He stepped outside and zipped the tent shut.

In the darkness beyond the canvas, I heard calls of the wild that night—the squeak of a Styrofoam lid, the rattle of an aspirin bottle and the pop of a carbonated beverage.

Resurgent Perspective, Part 1

I knew I was in trouble when my own dad called me by my last name. Along with being my father, he doubled as my baseball coach. I had just made a disastrous baserunning decision and was thrown out at third, ending not just the game, but the season. I had squelched my team's chance at our Little League championship. Tail between my legs, I sat down in the dugout beside my teammates as Dad expounded on my bungle for all of us to unmistakably hear. He gave a damn about my progress as a ballplayer. It was akin to my growth as a person.

My dad was well-qualified to address bonehead play. He played professional baseball from 1949 to 1954, mostly in the Cleveland farm system. He was signed as a left-handed pitcher, but early in his career a freak accident occurred in training camp. A teammate struck out, lost his temper and threw his bat. Dad was on the sidelines. In those days, there were no dugouts on the training fields. But my dad wasn't looking at the teammate and the bat hit him in his pitching arm. It never fully recovered and his pitching career ended. But my dad could still hit and Cleveland management put him at first base.

He never had an official at-bat in the big leagues. So he referred to time he might have spent in the majors as a "cup of coffee." It's a term for players who were called up barely long enough for a swig of joe. Dad's loose interpretation of that phrase dovetailed with some splashy tales he could tell. As a complement to being sonorous, my dad didn't hesitate to juice his baseball stories like a spitball.

Exaggeration was a big part of his shtick. He said he once hit a baseball so hard it rocketed between the pitcher's legs and slammed the centerfield fence on the fly. He told me of another time when he missed catching a line drive that was hit straight at him. It stung with such force that the label of the ball manufacturer transferred onto his skin. There was also a flame-throwing pitcher who struck out my dad on three straight pitches. After the third strike apparently crossed the plate, my dad turned to the umpire and argued that the last pitch *sounded* low.

A few teammates who became big leaguers were often a centerpiece of his stories. Most notable was his roommate in the minors, outfielder Rocky Colavito, whose arm strength was staggering. On a bet, my dad watched Colavito stand at home plate and throw a baseball not just over the centerfield fence, but completely over the bleachers and into the parking lot.

When Colavito was awarded Cleveland's "Man of the Year," he sent my dad a brochure from the banquet and inscribed it with New Year's greetings. For the eight-year-old I was, the sight of it was an eye-popper.

Ken Burns' epic documentary *Baseball* mentioned another of my dad's teammates. Harry Chiti was a weak-hitting catcher who was traded from Cleveland to the New York Mets, Major League Baseball's newest team at the time. The film described Chiti as so inept that he was the only player in baseball history to be traded for himself, sent back to the team he came from after just 30 days.

But my dad had other information about Chiti. He had a bazooka for an arm. He said Chiti could pick off runners at first base by throwing from a crouch and without looking or notifying the first baseman. My dad was regularly that first baseman and said he got tired of the ball hitting him in the groin by surprise then nursing the bruises.

My family moved from Philadelphia to the Chicago suburbs when I was six and Dad took me to my first major league game. It was between the Chicago Cubs and the Philadelphia Phillies at Wrigley Field. Walking up the grandstand ramp, I experienced a moment that only happens once. With each step, the field began revealing itself before my eyes, becoming increasingly larger. Finally, with it in full view, I stood beside my dad, agog at the greenery.

But that wasn't the only highlight Dad had planned. We had arrived well in advance of the game, back in the day when fans were allowed to watch batting and infield practice. Dad scanned the field for Phillies, then got up and told me to follow. I stumbled along under the stands looking around in wonder and trying to keep up with him. We stopped at a set of stairs and a walkway enclosed in a cage. Soon, Phillies players intermittently passed by and I realized we were right below their clubhouse. My dad called to one of the players and holy cripes they knew each other. He was utility outfielder Wes Covington. My first major league game and I met my first major leaguer.

While in the minors, Dad also met the legendary Satchel Paige. He said Satchel was reclining on a training room table covered across his middle with nothing but a towel and a guitar. They exchanged greetings and that was about all. But Dad said Satchel had the longest, skinniest feet he'd ever seen, with toes like broken carrots.

As a kid, these stories hooked me and I glommed for baseball history. In the process, I began hearing broadcasts and reading player interviews containing some of the same quips and embroidery as my dad's stories. I discovered that the story about the screaming liner between the pitcher's legs that hit the centerfield fence belonged to Satchel Paige. Unless my dad was the player who hit that ball against Satchel, this fable didn't originate with Dad. And for a while, I may have become jaded about the tales he'd tell.

Years later, I came upon a scrapbook my mom had compiled while dating Dad throughout his baseball career. They were high school sweethearts. It was loaded with delicate yellow clippings from Philadelphia newspapers and others in minor league towns where he had played. Reading how other people told his story woke me up. Maybe he really was *that* good. I experienced a resurgent perspective.

Two Philadelphia newspapers reported that he had been unanimously chosen by major league scouts to play in the state's annual all-star game. He "was selected by the American Legion as the second outstanding player in Pennsylvania." After his arm injury, another paper listed his season batting average at .371, stating, "Any player with such a clouting average is more valuable to the team playing every day." I also found that his Triple-A contract was signed straight out of high school.

Lee Remmel, the longtime historian for the Green Bay Packers, was a reporter for the *Green Bay Press-Gazette* when my dad played minor league ball with the Green Bay Bluejays. Remmel wrote a story exclusively about my dad's arm injury and the psychological effects of changing positions. Remmel called my dad the Bluejays' fiery first baseman and said of his dead arm, it "must be more than disheartening to one who has major league potentialities...to have his diamond progress retarded, possibly for all time through no fault of his own."

The best baseball book I ever read is *Bottom of the 33rd* by Dan Barry. It's based on the longest game ever played in professional baseball, a Triple-A game in 1981 that grinded out 33 innings. But it's not a play-by-play analysis. It's an account of the "players" in that game, who also included umpires, wives, announcers for the opposing team and the batboy's mom. Barry examined the disquieting reality of players who had spent five or six years in the minors, but had never been called up to the majors. It was about players like my dad.

Approximately ten percent of today's minor league players ever reach the majors for an appearance in just one game, that cup of coffee, much less sustain a career. In 1954, Major League Baseball only had sixteen teams, roughly half of the number today. Free agency was nonexistent and unless major leaguers were traded, they stayed with their team a long time.

Dad's chances of advancing to the majors eventually became microscopic and he had to reach a decision. He chose my mom, an engineering career and I showed up three years later. I never saw him play. But I have one of the uniforms he wore in the minors, a woolen hand-me-down from the majors with the major leaguer's name sewn into the neck label. And I have his stories.

For the record, Dad's lifetime batting average was .298. But the statistic that most makes me wonder "what if" was his pitching ERA, an impressive 2.03 runs per game. *What if* that bat hadn't hit him in the arm? It's the same "what if" that ninety percent of minor leaguers, or anybody, would ask. Sometimes life plays out in other ways.

The Truth about Magic

I looked right through it. Beyond bedtime on a December 24th sometime within my first eight or so years of life, I caught them red-handed. My parents, grandparents and great-grandmother had taken over Santa's responsibilities right there in the living room.

I had gone to bed but wasn't sleeping even though I wanted to. Considerable holiday enthusiasm and experience had versed me in bedtime protocol; Santa's arrival is quicker when sleep consumes the night. But my wandering mind decided on a stop to the bathroom. It was down a short hallway at the top of six steps in our split-level home. From there, anyone could see straight into half of the living room.

The stairway walls served as blinders, funneling the scenario directly into my line of vision. I saw my great-grandmother decorating the tree, Dad wrestling with some cardboard and a screwdriver on the floor, and an assortment of hands dipping into the cashew dish. Then I saw something else—every set of eyes seeing me see them.

I wasn't much of a detective back then. Analyzing evidence requires questions and I had none. I couldn't even come up with alternative facts like perhaps Santa was a little shorthanded that year, needed the help and my family pitched in. No, not me. Instead, my mind was a void to what I witnessed before my very eyes.

But for my parents, the jig was up and they stopped by my room one night afterward to fill me in. My reaction caught them completely off guard.

I couldn't widen my eyes enough to trough all the tears. I didn't want to disbelieve what I had treasured believing for so long. In that emotionally-crazed moment, I at least had the wherewithal to realize that the Easter Bunny was questionable, too.

To my parents' credit, I found they had tried to squeeze out another holiday of believer-days for me. Evidently, I'd begun to ask more questions than I thought. So the summer before the incident, our family made a visit to a nearby amusement park called Santa's Village. It was complete with an arena named the Polar Dome where I played most of my childhood hockey. Little did I know how ice-sheet technology of the day would play into our adventure.

Our focus was on a chat with St. Nick. He was said to live on-site seasonally and he brought his North Pole with him. The pole magically retained layers of ice even in hot weather. In reality, it was an eight-inch pipe about five feet high that arena maintenance had rigged with a water supply and freezer coils.

Santa also sported a real beard. When we met, he insisted I give his white whiskers a tug for good measure. Then we walked to the stable where I met actual reindeer, one in particular named Rudolph. I immediately detected that his nose wasn't red and asked about it. While such penetrating questions might have made Mom and Dad twitchy, Santa rebuffed it kindly. He told me Rudolph's nose only turned red in much colder temperatures, not unlike humans. The colder the temperature, the redder the nose, and it was ghastly cold where he normally lived.

So there. He said it. I believed it. That settled it.

This is what my parents did. They brought me one more Christmas Eve. And I still believe in the magic.

Navigational Purposes

By the time I left high school, I had the remainder of my life pretty much mapped out. Consequently, I should have been inducted into the National Hockey League Hall of Fame twenty years ago. However, that career plan began to siderail the summer after high school graduation.

Throughout childhood, I dreamed of playing goalie. But these years later, I can see how my mom and dad were in league to nudge me elsewhere. At the time, my parents purchased almost all of my equipment. It wasn't provided by a school or park district. However, the specialized goalie gear was extremely expensive. Just the leg pads and two gloves cost more than all of my regular gear combined. So they preferred me to stay out of the net.

They also wanted me to become a better skater. They reasoned that a goalie doesn't skate very much or very far. Goalies just stay at one end of the ice and often all alone. My parents even paid for figure skating lessons to improve my skills. Fortunately, that didn't last long. Unlike hockey skates, figure skates have a blade pick on the toe. During lessons, I'd habitually snag that pick on the ice and go sprawling rink-wide. To avoid permanent damage, they let me stop after a season.

I later found that a goalie is often the best skater on the team. That doesn't necessarily mean the fastest, but the one with outstanding agility, balance and footwork. But by the time college arrived, I hadn't spent one tick of the clock stopping pucks. I was a defenseman. So considering my experience and timeline, I had to accept that "defenseman" was my position for that career in the NHL.

Around our house, I must have chirped a lot about my aspirations. Eventually, my dad pulled me aside and tried to explain, "You can't just 'say' you're going to play in the NHL. It's not a regular job. It's a different level."

Thinking back, he was either looking to spare me disappointment or get me to shut up. Either way, I paid him no mind. What did he know anyway? He played professional baseball, but never made the big leagues. He only reached Triple-A. He taught me baseball. But this was hockey. We learned it together. Plus, I had more actual skating experience than him. Decision made.

In choosing a college, I had the foresight to not jump too far too fast. I recognized my early hockey days were around Chicago, not exactly a hockey hotbed like Canada or Minnesota. So for seasoning, I enrolled at a Division III school in Wisconsin. I'd play there for two years, then walk-on to the Big Ten campus in Madison where I'd make my mark. This also boded well for my joining the U.S. Olympic hockey team. I'd postpone college graduation by a year for the 1980 Winter Olympics. America didn't know then, but everyone knows now, about the miracle that team pulled off. Afterward, I'd head to the NHL. It could wait twelve more months.

No sooner had my parents dropped me off at college, than I went straight to the hockey coach's office to make my services available. But I found that over the summer, the local ice arena where the university team played had been sold and transformed into a supermarket. Without a nearby arena, the hockey program became a club sport. Fortunately, several colleges in the team's previous conference took pity on us and we played them when schedules would allow. It wasn't what I had envisioned.

The closest practice rink left something to be desired. It was outdoors, with ratty old boards and holes big enough to shoot volleyballs through. Errant pucks vanished behind them, their sound pranging car fenders parked along the curb. Ring three in a row and it scored a hat trick for the practice. One wind-ripping, twenty-below-zero night, the team lined up along the leeward goal line. Then for fun, everyone stood still and pointed their skates windward. Moments later, wind gusts began blowing us to the opposite end. This wasn't the fun I'd grown to love.

The speed of college competition was another eye-opener. It was blinding compared to high school and I had a hard time keeping up. My dad's point started coming into focus. Mostly though, I began discovering new academics I wanted to explore. I never did transfer schools.

My old hockey gear is now relegated to a Halloween costume if I need one. It's been bagged for so long, that when I unzip it, the aroma of my high school arena wafts out. Memories engulf me and I smile.

I've seen the Stanley Cup in person once in my life. It's hockey's highest prize. But since college I've made a pact with myself. Even if given the chance, I won't touch it. That might seem silly, especially to hockey fans who never played. And if they want to touch it, that's fine because they never transcended a magic veil. In a small way, by playing, I was given a glimpse of something deeper, of what's involved. To touch it would mean I earned it.

If The Cup and I meet again someday, I'll keep my hands in my pockets, content to just look. Dreams that don't come to fruition still have a navigational purpose.

The Soul of Place

I've had a recurring nightmare for several decades. In it, the woodland surrounding our family cabin is ravaged by housing development and becomes the poster child for urban sprawl. The nightmares started when my parents still owned the Cabin. When they passed away, I became owner for a short time, but now it's no longer mine. However, my nightmares have continued and the disturbance within them escalates as each installment unfolds.

The Cabin hosted laughter, celebrations of seasons, hunting stories, fires inside and out, and countless family gatherings. Its feng shui insisted that the outside come inside. As such, we occasionally harvested cattails from a nearby marsh and stood them to dry in an old wine jug just inside the front door.

The Cabin was a great place for doing uncle stuff. My sister-in-law brought her young family out to watch a Packer-Viking game on TV. The adults settled into libations while the kids revolved in and out the door. At one point, my five-year-old nephew breezed through and brushed against one of the cattails. Some of its fuzz fluffed airborne and levitated momentarily behind him. I asked him if he had farted. He smirked a, "No, I did not." So to legitimize my question I added, "Because there's one sneaking up on you right now." I pointed to the floating cattail dander and he turned. "See," I said, "That's what they look like."

His smirk instantly turned to panic and he clamored for escape. But the air current from his movement swirled and the fart chased him inquisitively out the door.

On the Fourth of July, my mom's unbridled patriotism made Uncle Sam look like a commie bastard. Arrayed in a cardboard tiara fashioned with red, white and blue foil, she'd perform spirited interpretations of the Statue of Liberty in live motion. With a crackling sparkler in each hand and a candle burning nearby for re-lights, she conducted Sousa marches that blared out the Cabin windows from the eight-track player inside. She didn't quit until every sparkler in the box had fizzled. The sight of it was enough to make a wood thrush roll off-perch.

The Cabin had a soul of its own and nurtured our dreams. It woke me to recognize I had fallen in love with DyAnne, my wife-in-the-making during our early days there. By her account, I was a little tardy in coming around. But infinite walks with her down the pine-scented lane, rain, shine or snow, had an effect on me.

Finally, when Mom and Dad were up for a visit, we took a bottle of champagne to the Cabin and announced our engagement. Mom cried. We expected nothing less. But Dad thought I was joking and walked outside to do something else. I had to fetch him back and tell him it was for real. Then he was all loud and joyous with us.

The Cabin was sheltered between modest hills on a curved road two turns from the main highway. The anticipation of reaching it peaked at the sight of a neighbor's small white house on the first bend of the blacktop. Especially after a troubled week, stress began rinsing away.

The house belonged to an older bachelor who Dy and I befriended not a minute too soon. His intriguing eyes reminded us of Rodney Dangerfield. We'd known who he was for a couple of years and exchanged friendly small-talk on occasion. His mother was an opera fanatic. His father played football for the Pittsburgh Steelers. Our friend's tastes sided with his mom and her opera. Once, he'd stopped over and by chance mentioned he'd never been inside the Cabin. I was more than surprised and properly ashamed—never again.

Get-togethers thereafter became habit. He'd bring the pork loin and we'd provide the brandy and cider. He liked using his cinnamon stick as both cocktail stirrer and Tiparillo when pontificating and emphasizing philosophy. We'd sit around the outdoor fire at dusk listening to turkeys fly to roost, muffled wingbeats like plastic garbage bags being shaken open.

Throughout life, his primary occupation was as a handyman. He was a wizard with machine tools and small engines. Our ancient lawn mower was his specialty. We gave him the motto, "If he can't fix it, it ain't broke."

He had two cats who lived into their twenties. But with that came his inevitable acceptance that their family as they had known it in this lifetime would need to conclude. He sent them to the afterlife together so one wouldn't have to be without the other even for a little while.

When he told me, he was so distraught that he leaned his hand on my shoulder at first, then fell into a full hold and sobbed. He had a hell of a clinch from a lifetime of turning wrenches and compassion for others.

Around that time, Dy and I had to make the same decision for one of our cats. But shortly afterward, he called the house where we lived in town and announced, "I've got your new kitten."

We came to find that he also claimed two of our kitten's siblings for himself. That meant more brandy and cider, another fire and extensive discussion on reincarnation. That kitten was our cat for sixteen years.

My parents didn't realize how close we had gotten to him. When Dy and I eventually moved to northern Minnesota, four-hundred miles away from the Cabin, we only returned twice. About a year after our move, my folks called with news that another Cabin neighbor found him in bed one day. He had passed away in his sleep.

My memories of the Cabin and surrounding area are still as crisp as if I'm actually there. I can still smell its earthy must, hear the creaky oven door open and close, see the two-foot artificial Christmas tree that we left up year-round to double as a nightlight.

In my nightmare, unfamiliar neighbors freely trespass on the Cabin land. They show complete disregard for our solitude and display a sense of entitlement to whatever is there. The formerly dense woods on the hilltop behind the Cabin have been gutted and I can see a road on the other side from a mile away. Sidewalks and culverts have replaced deer trails. The undersides of the few remaining tree branches reflect light from a convenience store just over the rise.

Maybe my nightmares have given me a heads-up. But I have no desire to return to the Cabin anyway. Its soul has quelled my nightmares and I've come to terms with our physical separation. If it has changed, I don't want to see it. Treasured memories take me forward.

Secret Fishing Hole

I'd like to think I'm pretty good at keeping confidential matters under wraps. But sometimes I've gone overboard and actually kept secrets from myself. That's what happened with my marriage proposal to DyAnne. I'd been moseying through our relationship for so long that the voices of the Universe basically had to club me over the head. Once I woke up, asking her to marry me carried such significance that I wasn't going to let it slip by without some fanfare. I kept that to myself, too.

The day I proposed started with plans for a trip to our secret fishing hole. But first I had to gather supplies for my three-phase operation. Components included an old hockey stick; a new Styrofoam minnow bucket; an oversized fishing bobber; tangled fishing line; two greeting cards; a freezer bag; and a rose. A bottle of Cold Duck and a cooler went without saying.

The day was sweltering hot. By early morning, humidity was so thick it curled calendar pages on the wall. Our secluded spot was at a nearby river where we fished from shore. I arrived there alone and strategically placed my items. For Dy, the occasion would be like a scavenger hunt resulting in a catch I hoped she'd find a keeper. I had pre-written one sign and two cards that gave directions to each mystery location. They contained inane little clues understandable only to us. Suffice it to say, the wording was heavily influenced by Monty Python's Flying Circus.

I nailed the sign to the hockey stick. Then I took it down a wooded trail and hammered it into the ground where we usually hid away for pitstops. I figured that as afternoon progressed, Dy would surely come across it.

Next, I slid the appropriate card into the freezer bag, sealed them inside the minnow bucket and covered it in brush near the sign. When the time came, I'd wander into the woods, sneakily set the bucket afloat in the river, then snag it back again where we fished a few yards downstream. For this phase, I trusted that the wind and river current would not carry the bucket too far from shore. Otherwise, I might have accidentally asked whoever found it downriver to marry me.

Phase-three was the gem—the bobber. It contained the actual proposal. That meant no joking with my phrasing on the card. I opened the bobber in advance and cut the card edges to fit inside. Then I nestled the rose on top of the card and taped the bobber back together.

From there, I maneuvered my truck under a tree branch, stood on the tailgate and hung the bobber around the branch with fishing line so it looked to be tangled in the tree. Then I drove off hoping the secret would hold just a little longer.

On paper, my scavenger hunt progressed from the sign to the bucket to the bobber. But upon returning, I learned of some design flaws, not the least of which was Dy's general disdain for scavenger hunts. The miserable heat also did nothing to boost her spirits for such folly. Plus, our quiet fishing spot had been invaded from across the river. Hidden behind the tree line, a highway construction crew was piledriving bridge abutments in rhythmic cacophony. No sooner had we arrived, than Dy suggested we leave.

With my plan on shaky ground, I faked a pitstop down the trail and returned with news about "some crazy sign back there." She went for a look, but rather than recognizing I was up to something, she got scared. She thought we were being watched.

Somehow, I convinced her to stay. But I had to keep the plan moving. So I told her I needed to dig up a few more nightcrawlers back by the sign. I reality, I dug out the minnow bucket and set it in the water. It floated about five yards. Then it wedged under a cluster of branches just above the water's surface. I grabbed a dead twig nearby and poked the bucket into the current.

When I returned to Dy, the bucket was already coming through. I mentioned it looked new and worth keeping, but Dy told me not to bother. It had drifted beyond the reach of our fishing net. I reaffirmed there might be something valuable inside and plunged into chest-deep water like a golden retriever.

Back on land and dripping wet, I opened the bucket and handed her the card inside. She read it, glanced at the bobber in the tree above the truck, then insisted on getting the hell out of there. Proposal crumbling, I said, "I think I know what this is about. Let's do what the card says." I climbed on the tailgate, untwined the bobber and gave it to her.

Tears started flowing but words didn't. *Well, way to go*, I thought. *First, I scare her. Now she's gonna say no.*

Truth was, she just couldn't speak at the moment. Finally, she nodded, *Yes*. And we broke into the Cold Duck.

We still have the rose, the cards and the sign. The hockey stick has been relegated to a cross-brace for our kicksled. The minnow bucket started smelling a little rank after a while, so we got a new one.

Over three decades later, we still consider that day our true anniversary. It was when we made our promise to each other. Formalities and ceremony beyond that were just paperwork and dancing.

Voices of the Process

When asked about how he writes songs, Tom Petty said he didn't really know. He described it as a very real magic that he has to wait for if he's lucky enough for it to happen. True to his humor and semantic dexterity, he explained it by comparison.

"It's kind of like an orgasm," he said. "You don't know how you did that."

Not knowing how or why something happened is the core of magic. It tickles the inexplicable, but it's no less real. For me, writing is more than putting words, sentences and paragraphs on a page. It's a magic place inside my head. While I'm there, writing process takes precedent over final product.

In the physical realm, no one is beside me while I'm on one of these excursions. But I'm never alone; I have visitors. In our culture, their identities vary by name: angels, spirit guides, intuition, visions, hunches and the like. I just call mine The Voices. They're a well-intended, playful bunch, but with a deeply serious, nurturing side and crosshair accuracy. When we throw in together, they buffet me with mesmerizing scenarios and provocative phrasing. I can't get enough.

But writing stories is also like reading a spell-binding book or watching a beguiling movie for the first time. I don't know what's coming any more than the next person with a box of picture-show popcorn in their lap. I have to wait for the page turn or scene change. Then it pops into existence and finds physical form. But with writing, there's the added appeal of somehow being a collaborator in its creation. I'm simultaneously audience and writer.

This process isn't always quiet and peaceful. There are times when I've decided to wrap up a writing session, but The Voices run on like an old jalopy that won't shut off. They steam and blurt next paragraphs, concealed metaphors and character quirks. This can go on for hours, as if they're saying, "C'mon, just one more…If it's okay with you, that is. We were on a roll here." I can't get mad at them because we have a blast. And when we finally reach a stopping point and I re-read whatever splashed across the page, I'm often baffled—I didn't come up with that. Sometimes I wonder how much credit I should receive after writing something…or if I did *any* of it on my own.

A person doesn't have to be a writer or artist of any kind to discover this magic. It's the fabric of any creative endeavor that's available in every life circumstance. Scientists, teachers, chefs, automobile technicians, detectives and athletes are all in on it. However, recognizing it before it slips away can be a challenge. I ought to know by now to trust The Voices. But sometimes I go off in unproductive directions. But better that than not at all.

As best I can discern, imagination is the portkey between the realms. The act of writing doesn't involve a lot of science, other than perhaps the nuts and bolts of grammar and mechanics. But elements like style, pace, sequence or just the germ of an idea to get me started, reside in the magic realms. I think the trick is paying attention to life and turning the rest over to imagination where The Voices can get at me.

Scribble down those alluring observations, solutions, possibilities, and goofy or profound idioms that mysteriously channel their way from head to pen. Then, believe in the magic and see who or what shows up. As Petty said, "Just put your antenna out and something might come in…at the strangest times… But to ignore the muse is just downright impolite."

The lines are open. Your Voices await your call.

Seasons & the Natural World

Collaboration of the Realms

I spit into a test tube, then sent it through the mail to a laboratory somewhere. When returned, the analysis would supposedly tell me about my ancestry. I don't profess to know a lot about science nor do I wish to. I'm a words person. I find more fun in bewilderment about how the physical world works.

But I'd been having hunches that my family's recollections of our history had gone awry. I was told English and German were the dominant influences. No one had ever mentioned Celtic clans in our lineage. But by chance, I came upon our family name above a house doorway in a photograph taken in Wales. So I took a chance and let science have a say. Unless my test results traced me directly to the Buddha, there might be some truth to it.

My spit test returned and confirmed my suspicions. It indicated mostly Celtic heritage and no German in sight. With physical documentation behind me, curiosity lured me further and became a spiritual journey.

Additional research tickled my excitement. I discovered a sport originally from Scotland called caber toss. Basically, the game features men dressed in skirts who throw telephone poles from between their legs. At first, I assumed such creativity resulted from too much whiskey laying around. Caber poles can be twenty feet long and weigh one-hundred-fifty pounds. Competitors balance the pole upright in cupped hands. Then they run with it, gaining thrust, and heave the pole so it over-ends a full rotation and falls away from the tosser. The sport has also expanded to include women's events.

Even more intriguing, are the thinkers with finesse among the brute strength of my people. Caber toss emerged from pragmatic purpose. When old-time lumberjacks needed to cross narrow gorges or streams, they threw logs across the chasm to form bridges. The objective in caber toss is not about how far the pole flies, but about the position of the pole after it lands. Poles angled closest toward twelve o'clock—the straightest bridge across the stream—receive the highest score.

As I dug deeper, I found that the Celtic flair for fashion, the kilt, is the likely precursor of conceal-to-carry permitting. Warriors of the day customarily hid weapons under their kilts. But kilts were multipurpose attire. They provided protection from weather, served as camping blankets and were emblematic of wealth, status and the casual man-about-town.

Celtic cosmology appeared to me in the form of a calendar carrying a thirteenth month. Though several cultures have developed thirteen-month calendars, the extra Celtic month lasted only three days, from October 31st through November 2nd. It coincided with their designation for Allhallows' Eve, or Halloween, All Souls' Day and Day of the Dead. To my surprise, of the many days in a year, I was born within the Thirteenth Month. This was surely a sign. I was being beckoned into the mist.

According to the Celtic lunar calendar, Allhallows' Eve is the transition from the old year to the new. For early agrarian families, it also marked the end of the growing season and hunting became the primary method for acquiring food. With the arduous work of planting and harvest complete, country folk embraced celebration and appropriate mischief. But they didn't forget gratitude. Farmers turned their fields and remaining crops over to the Divine and to their departed ancestors.

Celtic legend maintains that the separation between the spiritual and physical realms is most permeable on Halloween night. Ancestral spirits can more easily communicate with their living kin to offer encouragement and caution. In response, descendants who perceive those ancestral voices are called to kind-hearted action on the ancestors' behalf. The living are also invited to examine their intentions and desires, and request help from those in other realms to initiate positive change. The realms look after each other.

In her book *Herbal Rituals*, Judith Berger describes the thirteenth month as a three-day pause. It's as basic and necessary to human spirit as the physical pause between inhaling and exhaling. She suggests that taking conscious interlude during this three-day void in the year can help people respond to the unknowable, and to uncover hidden treasures of the Earth. Notably, this awareness isn't revealed through the rational mind, but through the soul.

I've developed a tradition for these three days. I set aside more time than usual to deer hunt. However, it's not primarily about bringing venison home. I go to a place where spirit takes precedent over natural science. For the record, I don't pretend to have had thunderous epiphanies. Instead, I experience quiet like I've never heard before. It stills the clutter in my head and requests me to listen.

The visual world nudges me, too. Toward the end of each hunting day, a curtain seems to materialize at the far reaches of my sight. The curtain is darkness. Objects I could see previously are shrouded. As nighttime deepens, the curtain gradually cozies up to me, so close that I want to reach through it. And I wonder, *What's watching me from the other side?*

Whenever a deer comes my way during hunting, to my thinking, it's the deer's choice, not mine. If it seeks passage to the other side, that's a silent agreement between its soul and mine, and no other.

I was determined to pass up a deer that had stopped in front of me. It stood broadside, repeatedly circled a few times, then stood again as if insistent on staying. After several minutes, I was finally convinced to shoot.

I later found that most of the venison was edible. But during processing, a separate wound was discovered on one of the deer's haunches. It had festered and the deer had been living with gangrene. I didn't know it when I shot.

In providing me food, the deer no longer suffered. It was our agreement. I was being looked for and looked after.

Raven's Hymnal

Snow keeps no secrets. It seemed in a gossipy mood last hunting season and helped me determine where deer had been traveling when I wasn't around. All the better for adjusting to their preferences. As suspected, one of my stands was in a good spot, but maybe too good, just ten yards off a deer trail. I'm thinking I might tuck it back more into the woods.

One day last year, two deer walked near another of my stands when I was actually there. It was like a celebrity sighting. Somehow, we closed the gap between our distances in everyday life and I caught a glimpse. I never saw their bodies in full all at once. But a few windows among the branches offered good views when they came through. There was too much brush between us for shooting and little did they know I was there.

Throughout that day, the snow that was caked on pine boughs began losing its grip. It slid off in giant, dusty puffs that never quite hit the ground but went floating adrift on the wind. By late afternoon, the sun backlit the trees, making hundreds of twig formations all over the forest look like crystal webs tinted with orange.

I actually heard the change of seasons, too. Ice was morphing from its early-season skin and setting up more deeply on the nearby lake. The first sound of it was so loud it snapped my head in its direction. Then it happened again in the same place. Eventually grunts and pops came from everywhere, pin-balling across the lake. I tried to mimic its sound vocally. It was kind of hollow or throaty, yet not quite a "gwump." It ended with a lilt or uptick, maybe a "hush." I couldn't quite get it, so I stopped.

As a kid, I never sang out loud when I was in church and I'm not any different in this church. I'll let the ravens cover the vocalizations. They can imitate anything. I'll bet it's already in their hymnal.

Good Hunting?

I met a father, son and labradoodle on the logging road where I deer hunt. They were grouse hunting and I was laying groundwork for deer season. They lived in the Twin Cities and, as hunters will do, we immediately started discussing the prospects for harvest. The dad asked me if deer hunting was any good in the area. My first response was "no." But it wasn't to keep them from showing up at my deer stand two weeks later.

Initially, my answer was based on what I estimated to be their definition of good deer hunting. So I talked of deer numbers. By comparison across the state, we don't have that many deer up here. There's not a lot of farmland in a boreal forest.

But it set me to thinking about what's meant by "good deer hunting." As verbs go, dictionary definitions of "hunt" include: to search carefully; try to find; or pursue game for food.

Oddly enough, "pursuit" sometimes means standing still in silent observation hoping deer come my way. In those circumstances, I pursue places where deer might likely pass by. However, once I become familiar with an area, I feel like a welcome guest and even share some laughs with the hosts.

Nothing is more basic for reaching those places than boots. They're the first line of comfort between earth and human feet. Unfortunately, my hunting boots have become a little dodgy over the years. So I spontaneously tested a crack in one of them by submerging it into a swamp puddle. After a few seconds without leakage, and no hand from beyond the grave grabbing for my ankle, I stepped back to leave. But suddenly, my other foot dropped through a tangle of tree roots and I sank to mid-calf.

When I pulled my foot out, the boot didn't come with it. The roots had it in their grip.

So much for silent observation. I laughed like hell. I had warm, dry feet, plus this new story to tell. That's good deer hunting.

On another occasion, a red fox trotted across my line of vision as I walked to my deer stand, then stopped inside some brush. I didn't have my camera, but we spent time sizing each other up. He stared and I gazed. His rust-red fur, fluffy white jowls and penetrating eyes were framed by twigs in the foreground. I needed no camera. That picture will be mine forever. Searching for deer put me in a position to see him. Our extended eye contact in that moment was good deer hunting.

Every so often, when the moon is feeling mischievous, she'll sneak up on me by surprise. Walking from my deer stand after dark, I approached an old logging site that was surrounded by the rest of the forest. As I passed into the clearing, the moon's light blindsided me like a flashbulb. She's done this before: a cloudless sky, tree shadows stretched across the gravel road and I could have read a book in her radiance. Of all the symbolism the moon casts, this recurring treasure was a reality of place and season—good deer hunting.

Right-Brain / Left-Brain

Red squirrels get a bad rap. But I'll admit their reputation is somewhat justifiable. They steal seed from bird feeders, ransack garden sheds, invade garages and bully grey squirrels. I've also noticed they get kind of mouthy during deer season, pealing off shrieks of staccato chirps while I try to sit quietly waiting for deer. I can only imagine how many times they've blown my cover. They're the whitetail's narc.

But that's just human perspective. For me, if the hunting day starts to drag after staring at the same landscape for hours on end, I can count on red squirrels for a pick-me-up.

Red squirrels are robust little eaters, especially regarding picnic-style nutrition. I watched one buzz through a pinecone like it was corn on the cob. Particles flew everywhere, pinecone shrapnel sprayed as if from a wood chipper. When it reached the far end, it sped back to the front end like returning an old-fashioned typewriter carriage.

During another sit, I caught sight of two red squirrels who got sideways with each other on a tree branch about fifteen feet up. They squabbled and slapped each other silly until they lost their grip and free-fell to the ground. Their bodies hit milli-seconds apart with two compact thuds. It knocked the wind out of me just watching it. I thought they'd be injured or dead. But neither broke stride and they chased each other over a log and up another tree.

When a day gets slow, every deer hunter has their own repertoire for passing time. I have a close friend who's a wildlife biologist and seemingly a left-brained thinker. I'm fascinated with how his scientific mind works, especially regarding tedium. He also has a thing for databases. However, not all are exclusively for wildlife analysis. His level of sophistication encompasses spreadsheets for wines, cigars and Wisconsin supper clubs.

Having devoted most of his life to studying the natural world, his go-to resources for biding time in the woods are everywhere. He often deer hunts from a ground blind and sometimes he'll text me photographs from his "classroom in a hut." At the end of a hunting day we compare notes. Last fall he found two different aspen leaves on the ground, quaking and bigtooth. He arranged them on his thigh, snapped a photo and sent me the picture with an explanation.

His first response to doldrum opted for physical, scientific observation. My first response leaned toward behavioral potential and concocting a story. I texted him that the excitement of my sit included a couple of red squirrels who showed up at the entry flap of my blind carrying banjos.

The differences in our right-brain/left-brain relationship have benefitted me over decades and I take his tips seriously. On my next trip into the woods, I looked for quaking and bigtooth aspen leaves.

Arts and sciences aside, we're on the same page regarding our desire for actual experiences in the outdoors. While nature photographs and documentaries are nice, they're still virtual. They don't sit us directly among real wild animals, float aromas of dew-drenched pines and expose us to whatever weather Mother Nature conjures. For both of us, the closer to firsthand experience, the better.

Through him—whether he's aware of it or not—I've learned that knowing the names of species is an additional way of encouraging closeness. The bird isn't just any bird when it's called a "grouse." The tree isn't just another tree when it goes by "aspen." Species also have names for their parts that makes them unique. "Quaking" aspen leaves differ from "bigtooth" aspen. A grouse has a "crop" where it stores food for later digestion, inside which might be "aspen buds" and "catkins." Call these by their names and become more intimate with the woods and its inhabitants.

My hunting buddy has also stupefied me with physiological insights. For instance, the heartrate of thirteen-lined ground squirrels in hibernation can be as low as two beats per minute. Its respiration is one to three breaths per minute. At those rates, my right-brain would get bored counting so few breaths just for the sake of some science. It's counterproductive to my woodland entertainment. But his method of teaching sticks with me in a way that classroom instruction sometimes doesn't.

I sat on my hunting bucket for the last day of deer season, no ground blind around me. As soon as I had settled, snow came down in wet flakes. No complaints. Clothing was my shelter for the day. But unlike in my ground blind, I could see in every direction just by turning my head.

Without warning, a red squirrel unleashed a scream a few feet behind me above my head. It about knocked my hat forward. I spun and saw it: elbows back, chest thrust forward. Then it looked me straight in the eye and let fly another extended wail just to make sure there was no mistaking who done it.

Such was its chutzpah—or maybe curiosity—that it frittered around for hours. I think it was trying to figure me out. At one point, it came in so close I could have touched its nose with the tip of my boot. It froze at my feet. This time, though, I wasn't interested in a banjo story. This felt like a microscope.

When it stood to examine me, I could see "it" was a "him." His unblemished fur had a tight comb, short and well-trimmed like he'd just come from the stylist. The chestnut-red along his back blended downward into a rusty-grey from his shoulders to his chunky haunches. Maybe he was experiencing some anxiety with my presence. I watched his ribs lift and recede steadily with each breath. And I started counting.

The Fox & the Turtle

A hatchling turtle poked his nose into October, clawing his way out of the nest where his mother laid him. He was a snapping turtle with a shell smaller than a golf ball. DyAnne and I barely noticed him as we walked down to the bank of the river.

We checked the hole he came from and found it littered with destroyed eggs. Some other animal had their fill over-easy and the little turtle was the only survivor.

Since we were probably headed in his direction, we considered giving him a lift. For a snapper that size, it wouldn't have been hard or dangerous.

In May, female snappers crawled across our yard looking for a place to nest. One particularly large mother crept over rocks without ever seeming to break stride. She was like a slow tank, muscling her way forward and nothing got in her way. Such moxie does not go without ballyhoo in our book, so we gave her a name. We called her "Wheels."

Naming wild animals is anthropomorphic as all get-out, but we do it anyway. It's fun, though it can come at a price. By ascribing human names or characteristics to nonhuman things we can accidentally con ourselves into believing that the natural world views life as we do.

Wheels often came close enough to our house for us to study the details of her prehistoric body. Her stair-step tail ridge looked like something from The Flintstones. She'd take a break from her nest search and blink back at us peacefully.

At the same time, we were mindful of being on the business end of her mouth. Stories and bar talk have turned snappers into legends. There's the popular, "If a snapper grabs your finger and you cut off its head, it'll still be clamped to that finger when you reach the emergency room."

A snapper's size rarely goes without embellishment: "heads like footballs, shells like garbage can lids." In reality, Wheels had a head more like a softball and a shell like a hubcap.

Judging by the destruction in the nest, there's no wonder why snappers lay twenty to eighty eggs, only to have a few pull through. Up to ninety percent of their nest can be destroyed by common predators. And though hatching in October is not typical, it's not unheard of. Our little friend was not some renegade trying to prove a point.

The female turtles worked so hard just to navigate their way around our yard, it didn't seem fair that so many offspring should perish. But therein lies the lesson.

The main predators of turtle nests are racoons, skunks and fox. Sure enough, there were a few foxes nearby and we caught one with its paw in the cookie jar swiping turtle eggs.

Actually, we liked having foxes around, too. As with the mother turtle, there was one physical standout. He was a sleek, puffed-chested, gun-slingin' kind of specimen that seemed to embody a character from a Hollywood western. We called him "Sloan."

So now we had made friends with two species who were at odds with each other. Anthropomorphism was rearing its head.

One day, in broad daylight, we pulled into the driveway and saw a curled up, red lump in the yard by the porch steps. We drove closer and even got out before it raised its head. It was a fox, but it wasn't Sloan.

This fox had mangy fur and an emaciated body with xylophone ribs. When it sat upright, its eyes wouldn't focus and it swayed lightly from side to side like seaweed in the ocean.

It also didn't act like a fox. It had no fear of us. When it walked away, it was just for a few steps. When we went inside, it came back to where we had stood.

We watched it try to stalk a bird nearby. But the fox stayed in the open with no apparent knowledge of how to use cover. We figured it would be lucky to live through the night. We didn't name it.

We could only guess at the reason for the fox's condition. Starvation was obviously part of it. Disease and an inability to hunt could have been in the equation, too.

It was pitiful to see, but it got us to thinking—who gets to win, the fox or the turtle?

As we looked at the hatchling's tiny shell, it was hard to believe he'd attain legendary size. Just living until he could plunk into the river was chore enough, much less surviving the dangers he'd experience in the water.

We were impressed with his robust attitude, scraping out of a hole, making his way homeward in October. So I leveled off the incline to give him an easier shot at conquering his hill. But maybe I shouldn't have meddled even that much.

A few years ago, the snapping turtle status in Minnesota was listed as a "special concern." Helping the hatchling to the river probably wouldn't affect their population. But maybe there was some other species that needed the turtle out in the open for its own survival, like a racoon, a raven or a pitiful fox.

The original version of this story appeared in the Timberjay *newspaper, October 13, 2007*

Reciprocal Spirit

I made a purchase that was like a puppy following me home. My investment was a brand-new, eight-horsepower outboard motor. Honestly now, it was insistent that we spend our lives together. Oddly, our relationship began with a flaw from the factory that immediately saved me two-hundred bucks over the counter. Then it became priceless over its lifetime.

The flaw was a cosmetic hiccup—the motor's cover was mislabeled. Instead of reading eight-horsepower, it said six-horse. Though missing just two horses, the oversight evidently caused buyer reluctance and the motor was stored at the marine dealership for over a year until I got there. Not to be swindled, I called the manufacturer hotline and checked the horsepower with its serial number. The numbers added up. This outboard and I were meant to be.

Just weeks after that, I added a johnboat and trailer, then got married the following year. My wife DyAnne and I took the whole package with us on our Canadian honeymoon and the stuff of memories began.

We kind of knew we were a gossip target at the resort. Our little eight-horse motor—which said six—was perceived as somewhat underpowered for the expansive lake surrounding the area. The flatbottom boat was also seen as more for shallows rather than tearing across a fathomless lake. Plus, anyone watching us return after a few outings knew we weren't catching many fish. Word spread and a group of guys enjoyed some fun at our expense.

Midweek, I caught up with the resort owner while he worked outside the guys' cabin. I inquired about renting a faster motor and boat for a daytrip to the far side of the lake. From inside, the group could easily overhear our conversation. The owner asked how our fishing had been even though he probably knew. I explained and he suggested we tip our hooks with live bait.

A voice boomed through the cabin window, "And then you put the bait in the water…!"

Guffaws broke loose and drowned out whatever he said next. Even the owner chuckled. Can't say I blame them. I thought it was funny, too. But I offered no apologies.

From that moment forward, we recognized something we subconsciously knew—we can see more of the world from a small boat. So that's what we did, explored places that aren't even in *National Geographic* documentaries. We putted down narrow, tree-covered backwaters too shallow for anything including fish. We nestled into weed beds and lily pads where only ducks and Jesus bugs reside, those insects nicknamed because they walk on water. Our motor, boat and trailer teamed up just to show us this majesty. The little outboard and I developed a confidence together that sometimes showed swagger.

I backed our boat down the ramp at a popular landing. The concrete pavement was wide enough to handle two trailers, one on each side of the dock. Dy and I had arrived just moments before a waterski boat with a massive motor pulled beside us. The truck towing it had barely stopped when every door sprung open and passengers evacuated into oblivion leaving the driver to himself.

After jackknifing the trailer on the ramp a few times, the driver straightened it enough to park and climb into the boat. I noticed his demeanor. He flung aside lifejackets and kicked inflatable unicorns across the deck. Then he shot me a glance, one of disdain, perhaps for being so small, a guppy unworthy of this landing. I'm not one to inflame already tense circumstances, so what I said next just snuck out.

"Wanna race?"

He stopped everything.

I had to come clean. "Okay…it says six, but it's actually an eight."

He threw his head back in a one-burst laugh and returned to his business.

The day was screaming hot. Dy and I motored up a creek away from the main channel to a favorite sandbar. Once there, we stepped out of the boat in midstream and laid in the water, just us and our cooler.

About an hour later, we heard voices from behind an island where the main channel circled back and joined our tributary. A boat crept toward us from around the bend, gradually revealing sunbathers lounging across its seat cushions. It came into full view. It was the behemoth from the boat landing. However, my race rival was standing alone in knee-deep water shoving his back against the transom. He was trying to free the belly of that beast from one sandbar to another.

Our humble eight-horse started discreetly and we slid away. Had the behemoth guy seen us watching, I think he would have been more embarrassed than if we actually had raced and my motor won.

The summer after my mom died, our boat and motor took my dad and I fishing. We toured through a rivulet carpeted with waterlilies and banked with pines against both shorelines. The aromas and sights tripped my dad's memory to family camping and he reminisced about my mom. Later in the trip, he struggled to tie a lure onto his fishing line. I looked away until he completed the knot that his Alzheimer's was short-circuiting. By midafternoon, the eight-horse shuttled us back to the dock with slow, steady reliance. I was in no hurry. It was the last time I ever fished with my dad.

Over time, the eight-horse also began shutting down, becoming unreliable beyond repair. Reluctantly, I traded it in. But it gave me a final serving. After thirty-three years, its trade-in value was half of what I originally paid. That calculated to twelve dollars per season. Today, one four-hour boat rental is four times that price.

I'm convinced that inanimate objects have a soul. From some ethereal place, they offer a reciprocal element of spirit and no cash-register discount can ever compete.

Points of Entry

Every so often I find myself biding time behind the steering wheel of an outfitter shuttle parked at an entry point to the Boundary Waters Canoe Area. It's kind of like a police stakeout to nab the perp. The shuttle and I lay back and become part of the scenery. The difference is that I'm there to pick up people returning from paddling trips in the wilderness.

If those groups are behind schedule, waiting can last a while. When I'm alone, I'll sometimes lower the shuttle windows and let pine fragrances waft inside as I read. Other times, the commotion of canoes and kayaks offers entertainment.

A Subaru pulled in front of me and interrupted my solitude. I closed my book and set it aside. The roof carrier on the Subaru was empty, but the car trailered a tri-hull kayak. Both the trailer and kayak were spotless.

A lone young man got out and walked a short way to the shoreline. For several minutes, he studied the water. He returned to his car, stood over the trailer straps holding his kayak and studied them, too. After several more minutes, he disconnected the straps, got back in the car and paged through a manual of some sort. Apparently satisfied, he got out again, lifted the kayak into an embrace and cradled it to the sandy part of the shore beside the dock.

Once back at his car, he opened its rear hatch, perused more gear, then sat down above the bumper. After some deliberation, he carried a double-bladed paddle to the kayak. He returned and rested. Afterward, he reached for a collapsible fishing pole that telescoped into the length of a wand. He stood up, walked it to the kayak and bungeed it in securely. One piece at a time, his operation continued.

An onslaught of Boy Scouts stormed in and tumbled out of their caravan like a regiment of Keystone Cops. One Scout in particular was the obvious authoritative figure of all-things aquatic. He was about fourteen. He strutted around the canoe trailer in mid-calf leather boots lecturing endlessly on high-grade fishing line and his capsize-free technique for loading canoes. Three of his deckhands removed one of the aluminum canoes from the trailer racks, plunked it to the ground, then grunted food packs, coolers and canvas duffels into it.

A group of four young women drove up just after the Scouts. They were teenagers, too, maybe just two or three years older than the boys, but they obviously knew their way around the wilderness. Nylon portage packs. Carbon paddles. Lifejackets. That was it; no extraneous gear. And they weren't afraid of getting wet. Without hesitation they marched into the water and floated two Kevlar canoes into place. Their name-brand footwear with the "hydrophobic mesh uppers" and "granite grip soles" performed as advertised online. They began loading.

Meanwhile, with two Scouts at each end of their canoe, the pontificator and his crew lifted it and shuffled toward the water. They traveled about ten yards before the canoe crashed back down. Gravel popped and cackled under the hull. It caught the attention of a Scout leader.

"What the hell are we thinking here, men?" he quizzed. Boys' faces looked at the ground. "Ya load it in the water, not on land!" he barked. He rolled his eyes and spotted the girls. "There!" he pointed, "Watch those girls and do it like they do!"

An old pickup truck bounded into the scene. A dented aluminum canoe with chipped camouflage paint stuck out the back of the truck bed. The landing was getting crowded. So I walked onto the dock to look for my group and figure a spot for them to land. But they were still nowhere in sight.

During all this hubbub, I'd lost track of the kayak guy. However, his boat had been moved onto the dock. I'm not much of a paddler, but even I could see that vessel was state-of-the-art stuff. Its seat alone had more comfort adjustments than a recliner.

When I turned to leave, I bumped right into him. This time he held an anchor in one hand and wore full-body neoprene. Electronics were connected all over him. The GPS strapped around one bicep, and an apparent depth finder on the other, looked like children's water wings. His Dick Tracy watch was arguably inflatable. On the chance he'd ever fall overboard, he'd either float or sink straight to Davy Jones' locker.

I admired his anchor. He explained its three-pound stainless construction could hold seventeen-hundred pounds. Plus, its E-Z Fold design provided optimum storage. But he was concerned that it wouldn't bite into the local lake bottoms.

Meanwhile, the man and woman from the old pickup slid the canoe off the truck. The man shouldered it and headed to the water. We smiled at each other as we passed. He was thin, sported a long grey beard, denim cutoffs and sandals. From the shuttle, I saw him meet up with the kayak guy and watched the body language between them.

The gentleman knelt down and looked under the kayak. He said something and the kayak guy nodded. The gentleman also examined the anchor, seat and GPS. He listened a lot.

Once back at his truck, he nudged his wife as she cinched their anchor bag closed. "It's like our old tri-hull bass boat," I heard him say. "More gee-gaws than my karma could handle." They chuckled and gathered the last of their gear. "His anchor cost more than this canoe, but he's concerned it won't bite into the local lake bottoms." He shook his head. "All that tech and he's afraid to get in."

They waved to the kayak guy as they pushed off shore. The girls were gone. Even the Boy Scouts managed to leave. The water ripples from everyone's departure had flattened. But the kayak guy stared at his boat and its upside-down image mirrored on the surface.

I found the spot in my book where I left off. But when I turned a page, I caught a glimpse of the kayak guy. He had ventured out, barely away from the dock, gingerly dipping the paddle blades into the water.

A Step Ahead

I watched someone slide what looked to be a shotgun out of its case. It came from the back of a pickup stopped behind a car on the side of the two-lane about a quarter-mile down. Both vehicles had passed me about a minute apart a few miles back. The car was in front, an older model with a missing wheel cover. The truck was in decent shape. As I got closer, a guy with the gun and two other people disappeared into the ditch.

A gunshot came moments later when I was a few yards from the truck's rear bumper. I crept by, lowered the passenger window and peered down. Two of them looked at me as they came back up the embankment. The third person was turned away and hunched over at the base of the ditch. The one carrying the gun waved me on and I knew to keep going. As I accelerated, I caught him in my rearview mirror returning the gun to its case and setting it back in the truck bed.

Ten miles farther from town, I came upon a guy standing alone on the roadside with a gun in one hand and a chainsaw in the other. His coat was smudged in several places. For this, I had to pull over.

There was no foreboding soundtrack in the background when I passed the people in the ditch. The guy with the chainsaw wore no maniacal goalie mask. But Hollywood and large-scale metro media has perhaps conditioned nonrural residents to think there should have been some sort of warning.

The movie *Pollywogs* by filmmaker Karl Jacob takes place in northern Minnesota where he was born and raised. During an interview on KAXE radio, Jacob explained that gun ownership and hunting were a natural part of his life. Guns were no different from any other farming and harvest tool.

Pollywogs includes a scene at a family reunion when three family members put away their firearms after a friendly round of target practice. Their discussion is focused instead on a divorce-turned-ugly, though not violent, for the main character. Little regard is given to the guns other than for safe storage.

Jacob described the scene as a practical screenwriting technique for characters to have a conversation that kept the plot moving. But after film screenings, particularly in New York and Los Angeles, he said many viewers reacted in ways he never expected. Some mistook the scene as a setup for a shooting to happen later in the film. Furthermore, he was surprised by how these viewers were confused or disturbed by the casual way this family handled guns.

Access to guns is a major issue in America. It is a fierce topic of debate among lawmakers. Laws defining gun safety and possession requirements are necessary components of gun ownership and ones I strictly follow. However, ownership responsibilities extend after gun legislation passes. And they start before those laws must be enforced and someone is held accountable.

In an op-ed for IndieWire, Jacob said the urban reaction to *Pollywogs* highlighted his need to write his next film, *Cold November*. The story reflects Minnesota's hunt-to-table culture and the pragmatic use of guns that's detached from current-day political conversation. It features a 12-year-old girl who experiences rites of passage during her first deer hunt. She's guided by a primarily matriarchal hunting camp comprised of her mother, grandmother, aunt and an uncle. That familial support and training help her navigate unexpected circumstances in the woods.

Several sixth- through twelfth-graders in our area schools compete in the Minnesota High School Clay Target League. As of 2021, the league has nearly thirty-seven-thousand shooters from thirty-four states. All participants are required to earn one of two firearm safety certificates. Many of those kids also hunt with their families under adult supervision.

Living on the edge of a wilderness doesn't automatically qualify us residents as backcountry stump-jumpers. But if that perspective feels murky, consider this—we tend not to shoot each other.

Our county is geographically larger than two New England states. According to sheriff's department records, over the past eleven years in the northern, rural region of the county, there have been just two incidents of one person shooting at another. Neither was murder. Compared to big-city standards, we bumpkins are a step ahead.

We can also piece together evidence and come up with a likely story.

I'm guessing the ditch people were recovering a deer hit by the car. Based on some blaze orange the men from the truck were wearing, I suspect they were grouse hunters who happened by the scene at a fortunate moment. Fortunate because the deer was wounded and the hunter with the gun mercifully put it out of its misery. I'm also pretty sure the hunter hunched in the ditch had begun field dressing it. One of those three people would take the deer to be processed for food.

That's what I saw. I've had enough similar encounters over time to condition my perspective. But in telling this story, I did something sneaky. I left out shreds of evidence earlier that could have validated reader suspicion. The blaze orange was missing. The missing parts are examples of how media can manipulate an image.

In the case of the chainsaw guy, I got to actually talk to him. His blaze orange coat was smudged with dirt and grime from working on his broken-down truck. It quit on him a mile back. I remembered seeing it parked down a side road. When he couldn't get it to run, he grabbed his gun and chainsaw, both encased, and started walking back to camp for help.

I gave him a ride.

Friends & Neighbors

North of Minnesota-Nice

A carload of conniving faces made several slow passes up and down our block a few summers ago. They were transfixed on something across the street in our neighbor's yard when our neighbor wasn't home. Eventually, they crept to a stop. Car doors opened and the pack stepped into broad daylight. The Georgia plates on the bumper belied the lone female passenger who spoke with the British accent. To watch them was to surmise furtive intent. Yet, something wasn't right with the picture.

These were obviously novice hooligans. They were dressed all wrong: shorts, sandals and t-shirts from a nearby resort. They shot each other self-conscious glances. They diddled street-side by a sign handwritten in plain English that said, "Free." And they stood bepuzzled beside a used but still serviceable fish house for when the lakes froze over. Basically, they didn't know what to do.

The apparent ringleader took charge, giving the shell of the fish house a quick once-over. But no sooner had they begun trying to collapse it, than our neighbor screeched into his driveway and jumped from his truck seat toward them. "Ya interested?" he called out.

Indeed, they were.

Come to find they were counselors at a local kids' camp in summer. In winter, they were students at the community college up the road that specializes in natural resources. Having arrived from parts unfamiliar with frigid, they were captivated with the notion of ice fishing. It required no casting, trolling or hundred-horse outboard. Just cut a hole in the ice and drop a line right through. The ice house was no more than a tent on a toboggan with a flap in the floor. Quite a find for these adventurous spirits from elsewhere.

After a sales pitch and set-up instructions, our neighbor dug out tie-down rope from his garage. Then he supervised cramming the fish house into the car trunk and sent them off, waving good luck.

Later in fall, two other of the group's outdoor classmates from the sunny South came upon another steal in similar curbside fashion—a power ice auger. It needed some repair. By early November, lakes had just a skin of ice on top, but weren't reliably safe, even for foot traffic. However, the sight of ice added to their excitement of fishing in winter.

They took the auger to the local marine dealer for a quick looksee inside the motor. Their questions and exuberance percolated over the sales counter—*Get that grinder going in a hurry*. It caught the ear of the woman writing the service order.

Time passed. Whenever one of the students phoned the shop inquiring about the repairs, they were fed a litany of excuses: the technicians hadn't gotten to it yet; it was still in pieces; parts were on backorder. The two wondered if it was because they weren't locals and they mentioned the continual runaround to their outdoor recreation instructor at the college. Finally, the instructor contacted the shop in their behalf.

"Yes, it is because they're not from around here," the service writer said. "Bless their enthusiasm, but if they have it too soon, they might fall through the ice. Let's wait another two inches and we'll put those parts back together."

Silence of the Lawns

DyAnne and I sat down in the backyard, each clutching a can of perfectly frosted Hamm's beer. For early June, the day was scorching hot. I had finished cutting our grass and reached a good stopping point for the day. All other yard chores would wait. We settled in for an evening of quiet inactivity and baseball on the radio.

No sooner had the cold sizzle of beer rinsed down my throat, than our neighbor's hired grasscutter fired up his supercharged ride'em lawnmower next door. The ballgame broadcast was swallowed beneath the roar, along with all conversation between Dy and me. As he bounced in the seat along our property line, he waved a "hello" and shrugged an apology for being so noisy late in the day.

Our neighbor came out. She flagged him down and the mower killed. As best we could discern from their exchange a backyard away, she wanted him to show up earlier in the day and provide a heads-up before he arrived. She also requested he not mow over some patches of wildflowers in the yard. But he argued for more of a golf-course manicure.

These landscaping differences somehow segued into debate regarding the use of fossil fuels versus sustainable energy. Though cordial, their volume escalated. When their political sparring came to an impasse, the grasscutter turned the key, shoved the mower into gear and grabbed his cell phone. From there behind the wheel, he dialed and began talking. Dy and I could barely hear each other and sat perplexed at how he could hear anyone while directly above the mower engine. I went to the fridge for more Hamm's.

At that point in summer, we felt comfortable enough to sit and admire the sunset behind the haze of distant Canadian wildfires. Drought hadn't become part of daily life. Fires hadn't become a threat. Lawnmowers hadn't gone quiet.

Other sounds echoed through the neighborhood as summer continued to cook. The thwack-thwack of an air-powered staplegun ricocheted off house siding from somewhere nearby. I tracked it down to a new garage being built two houses from our intersection. I moseyed to their backyard and was greeted with the aroma of freshly cut two-by-fours aligned on an unblemished concrete slab.

The following day, I wandered across the street to the neighbors who lived next door to the new garage. We stood beside each other, arms crossed with curiosity, and assessed the project's progress. Our gathering turned into a committee meeting. With the shingles being hammered down right in front of us, we determined that the garage was nearing completion. So we made noises for a type of christening, kind of like a barn raising or a "frolic" as the Amish call them. The only differences between us and the Amish were that Amish community members supply actual labor for barn raisings. None of us had lifted a finger to help with garage construction. As for the neighborly celebration, our scheme was more hijinks than reverence.

We devised a plan to round up items from neighborhood garages and pack them into the new garage before the owners could move their own stuff in. Anything that took up space would do: boats, dogsleds, leftover heating duct, old refrigerators, garbage cans, used toilets and especially lawnmowers. By then, nobody needed them anyway. As I walked home across our yards, I caught myself chuckling. I also heard the dead grass under my feet crunch like potato chips. When I stepped on a pine cone, it snapped like a walnut.

Our land of sky-blue waters was parched with thirst. Anorexic river and creek beds began showing their skeletons as the drought wore on. Water levels dropped, exposing boulders and logs normally hidden beneath running current. However, one neighbor viewed this as a moneymaking opportunity. He ventured across jumbles of river rock and driftwood, collected fishing lures that had gotten snagged, and resold them.

Wilderness outfitters don't come by cash so handily. Like farming, their income relies in part on weather. As the drought transformed the forest to tinder, new fires ignited haphazardly. Outfitting businesses re-routed guests out of harm's way, all to afford those visitors a pleasant escape from their everyday lives. At the same time, outfitters and their employees kept an eye on their own escape, one that would force them to pack up, evacuate their homes and pray they'd have an everyday life to return to. When the wilderness was eventually shut off to travelers, so was outfitter revenue.

The individuals on the front lines fighting those fires are the essence of "hero"—they know the dangers, but face them anyway. Surrounding communities have responded with overwhelming gratitude. They've donated so much food to firefighters that incident command centers no longer have indoor storage space. Overflow food has been stockpiled in the open, sparking a new problem—black bears looking for handouts. It's not the bears' fault for being hungry. The drought has decimated the berry crop in the forest and bears scrounge for food anywhere they can find it. But they've become nuisances at the command centers and crews have had to fend off bears in addition to fires.

Weeks have turned into months. Normally, I relish the smell of a campfire. But frequent wildfire smoke has made breathing a conscious task. Some rural residents have already had to evacuate. So the possibility of abandoning our neighborhood hovers like the smoke plumes to our north and south.

What I'd give to hear the sound of an aggravating lawnmower again.

A Course of Human Events

Early on a Fourth of July morning, hours before holiday festivities kicked into gear, I met a friend and his children as we walked across the grocery store parking lot. He was at the end of their family procession trooping toward the door. We exchanged local pleasantries about the day ahead, pretty mundane stuff, then went about our business.

I saw him again later that day. But this time, I about did backflips to attract his attention from the porch where I was standing. He was marching as a parent in the Little League contingency of our small-town parade. I bellowed his name over the heads of people lining the street. He turned his head my way then whipped tiny candy baseballs at me. It left me questioning myself.

I'm captivated by parades, but I'm not sure why. I see my friend often. The people I watch go by in a parade are the same people I talk to on the other side of the gas pump or run into at recycling. Yet, pointing and waving at them from the sidewalk as they walk down the middle of the street feels so much more worthy of overjoy than at the grocery store. This is the silliness of parades.

I've taken part in parades in a variety of capacities: spectator, participant, news photographer and backstage beverage operator. I've come to realize that the pageantry of the parade in Ely, Minnesota, would shame a Disney anniversary. It's why so many politicians show their faces and name-banners at the doings, glad-handing with the people. The less favorable among them—and they know who they are—walk the centerline of the street rather than run a gauntlet too close to curbside constituents.

During the wee hours of sunrise preceding the Fourth of July, spectators begin setting up lawn chairs to claim spots along the parade route. They can trust that those chairs will be there when they return. Later, they filter in with dogs in tow and coolers to the side. Behind them on the grounds at the local park, the canoe-portage races and backcountry tent-pitching competitions heat up.

Somewhere in the middle of this merriment, a suspense builds throughout the morning. Onlookers become preoccupied with their watches and time of day. What's to come only lasts seconds and those who are gathered listen more than look. Then instantly, muffled thunder crescendos to a deafening pitch as the flyover fighter jets from the One-Forty-Eighth Fighter Wing rip across the sky. Though their roar is audible moments in advance, they're in the next town by the time their tails vanish from sight.

Not to be outshined, Ely extends this excitement with a flyby of its own. A plucky floatplane brings up the rear, pontoons all aglimmer, and buzzes the park barely above the treetops as if intent on catching up to the fighter jets.

Flashing lights from the police cruiser lead the military color guard and the parade explodes to life with all-things North. Logging trucks loaded to the top scent the air with the spice of fresh pine. Snowmobile and ATV clubs showcase their customized chariots. Fish houses become floats. Participants in the street shower the crowd with an array of treats: candy, oyster crackers, packaged underwear and power squirts from water guns. Activists of opposing political factions are spaced at safe distances from each other.

The Ely Lawn Chair Drill Team delights spectators with a choreographed salute to backyard furniture. This slick legion of women snap, spin and flip aluminum chairs under arms, over heads and behind backs with the synchronistic fluidity of Olympic ice dancers.

The Ely Klown Band overruns the pavement from one gutter to another. They're an assortment of musicians dressed as clowns happy for a place to play. Post-high school ages are inconsequential to band membership. For my first Ely parade, I wasn't able to witness their performance. But those of drinking age came to me. I was behind the scenes bartending a solo shift when the lot of them busted through the door. They came for some quick-lube to make themselves funnier in public. I scrambled up and down the bar serving a couple dozen of these clowns.

Having paid my dues on the sidelines over the years, I finally worked myself into the parade. It resulted in getting cooked inside a rubber chicken suit on a sizzling day. I was the new guy at the radio station and management needed a sap to fill the role of "Chicken Man," the superhero from the old radio adventure series. Oddly, even in sweltering heat, there was something empowering about it.

Festooned in heroic feathers, I stood with my upper body through the sunroof of an SUV. Every so often, I'd duck below the roofline, lift my beak and gulp water. I'd pop up again, point at little kids and encourage bodybuilder poses. Some kids scurried behind their parents. Others flexed their muscles back at me. For a guy in a chicken suit, I was also reminded that many adults in the crowd had been sucking suds since breakfast. My chicken costume offered protection from debris that came my way like bottle rockets and beer cans. But in that heat, I wouldn't have minded if the cans were full.

Our founding fathers began the Declaration of Independence with the words, "When in the course of human events…" I wonder if events like the ones in our town are what they had in mind. Their courage and sacrifice were likely focused instead on developing basic democracy. Celebrating with hairbrained whimsy is just one of our indulgent freedoms that transpired later.

"Courses of human events" still play out around the world today in countries whose citizens would rather not walk down the middle of their main street being pointed at. I'll be mindful of that even if I never wear a chicken suit again.

Too Much in Common

Per capita, small-town residents know more fellow residents than city dwellers know their community members. While perspectives and political issues are conscious choices, by and large, a sense of community seeps into hearts and minds of small-town folk without decision or weighing the benefits. On the edge of the wilderness, it's a subconscious necessity that just seems to happen.

This principle extends to a variety of elements in life. For instance, it helps regulate behaviors like road rage. No matter how crappy someone drives in town, we're reluctant to cuss at whoever is behind the wheel.

We might know who they are.

On a cold winter night recently, residents showed up in droves at a performance by a hometown folk band to celebrate the release of their first CD. T-shirts, promotional pins, posters from previous show dates and stacks of their CD lined the concession table. Band members—who we already knew personally—happily circulated through the fanbase and autographed the liner notes.

The event was a playdate for the entire family, no babysitters required. Elementary school kids snaked their dance line between tables, chairs and ever-shifting pockets of adult conversations. One toddler became so enamored with the band that she broke loose on all-fours and made an appearance across the stage until Mom was able to whisk her aside. Pre-schoolers devised forts beneath the skirted banquet tables along the wall. Occasionally, the event center owner made a friendly pass down the line, lifting the fort walls and flushing out kids like grouse from a thicket.

For the adults, it was sharing stories face-to-face without Facebook. Laughter was audible, no need for emojis. Compassion was verbal and visual, not expressed through a frowny-face cartoon. Everyone was accountable for their words. While debate from people of opposing views could become impassioned, all were generally civil to each other. They have too much else in common.

In the North, winter-talk is obligatory. We had been making good ice throughout fall until that thaw hit in early December. A former co-worker at the party reminded me of the slush the thaw created and how it re-froze to cause dodgy ice. What's more, even at 20-below, water in some rapids areas can remain open, so be careful.

The band's CD took four years to produce. The final product was just part of the pleasure. The crowd was full of people versed in knowing devotion to a process and accomplishing a positive result for a cause. They included owners of established businesses; start-up entrepreneurs methodically crafting achievement; artists who have heard applause or won awards; polar explorers, wilderness guides and dogsled mushers who have physically struggled from here to reach there; and teachers who were among the first to mentor goals and dreams.

Looking out for each other invites a spectrum of scenarios. The CD release was festive. Similar events might help a neighbor pay medical bills or raise funds for the high school senior class trip to Washington, D.C. Other times, the support is less tangible but no less important. When the firehall siren screams into the sky, thoughts and questions turn to everyone involved. Fire? Car wreck? Thin ice? What will they need?

We might know who they are.

The Winter Stall

Numerically, February is the shortest month. Psychologically, it's the longest. It slogs along like a benumbed dimwit traipsing through the calendar. February owns all of winter. We might as well X-off all other months capable of unrelenting snow and temperatures that make ice, and call every bit of it "February," the 212-day month.

Winter has stalled and there's no end in sight.

For our region, February is that time of year when we're as winter-conditioned as we're going to get. Mere teens below zero is time-wasting chitchat in line at the grocery store. We've earned our bragging rights, even though Alaskans and Canadians snicker at our comparative intolerance.

I love winter under most circumstances. After a snowfall, nothing is as fresh-smelling and pristine-looking as pure white everywhere on everything. February recurs like a placebic joke to humor us until the fishing opener, a.k.a. Mother's Day. But even by the second weekend in May, ice sometimes isn't off the lakes and sideways snow isn't uncommon.

The early stages of winter at least have deer season and an assortment of holidays. That's when layers of snow begin to build, concealing remnants of autumn in their mortar. There's no remembering what all we'll find under it when it begins to melt. I once watched a raven extract a genuine treasure—a convenience store coffee cup. It was buried so deep in the snowbank that the entire raven disappeared momentarily while excavating. Then he popped up, cup rim clamped in his beak, all of which encircled his face. It appeared to block his vision, but he flew to the nearest tree and was obviously in no mood to share his espresso fix with incoming company.

We've had to put up snow fencing in our yard for the past several winters. We don't want to because it's a neighborhood eyesore. However, the fence isn't for blocking snow. We live on a corner that's near a snowmobile trail and our street is an artery to food and fuel in town. The fence is to discourage snowmobiles from cutting through our yard. But during some winters, it backfires; the snowbanks are so deep that sleds can drive over the top of the fence.

Let there be no mistake. I hold our area snowmobile clubs and training programs in high regard. They provide extras to the community like trail grooming for our sled dog race. But buzzing neighborhood properties is another case of the respectful majority taking a hit for the few who besmirch the sport.

Some of those same types also have an affinity for embankments. The snow mound on our corner is a good example. It's enough to make stunt drivers drool. Maybe I shouldn't plant this idea, but an open-throttle run up that snow ramp would shoot sled jockeys skyward and they could change the bulb in the street lamp.

Oddly, the corner stop sign has taken on a contrary purpose. The time-honored red octagon is sometimes viewed as a black-and-white checkered flag like the one at Daytona. Full-bore acceleration ensues. It had a dire consequence for one driver last winter—an unopened beer can ejected from his coat pocket.

When I retrieved it, I found the beer inside wasn't my brand. So I poured it out rather than chase down its rightful owner. But as the last of its suds glugged down the drain, I got to thinking. Our local radio station broadcasts notices for lost and found items. Perhaps I should have sent in an announcement about the forsaken beer can to see who came to claim it.

On second thought, let's not be hasty. If this trend continues, I could collect enough for a six-pack too enticing to resist.

Pockmarks in Plaster

All we wanted was a simple paint job. It lasted a year and a half.

Kitchens get my vote for amassing the most stuff in the functional living area of a home. From refrigerators to toothpicks, we jockeyed appliances and cupboard contents to other rooms around the house. Anywhere was legitimate relocation for anything. The microwave, a loaded rack of washed dishes and several utensil drawers found their way into the bedroom. We thought the temporary residence of kitchenware in unaccustomed places would last a day or two, depending on the project phase. But sometimes it turned into weeks and that didn't count when we reached good stopping points and could put stuff back in its usual place. We returned to those phases later and moved the same stuff a second, third and fourth time. In the process, we lost some parts, like a roll of aluminum foil we'd used just the night before. That one didn't even show up in the couch cushions.

There's no teacher like experience and I dip into that well frequently. I've done my share of home improvements throughout life, but could still use some work on my in-the-trenches technique. I do my homework and garner all the advice I can get. I try to listen with an open head and heart, and follow instructions to the letter. But my efforts continually collide with what I think I've learned and actual accomplishment.

I found that do-it-yourself YouTube videos can be misleading. Those experts in front of the camera have done the work they demonstrate since birth. They sling on plaster like Tom Sawyer whitewashing a fence. However, that isn't on my skill chart, so I repeated the putty-sand-wash procedure in a never-ending nightmarish loop.

Can't say I embrace that repetition. But starting over was my constant companion and integral to lesson retention. For instance, if a standard vacuum accidentally inhales even a small amount of water, the wet bag loses structural integrity. Then it splits and blows contents out the back end. It's good to catch this sort of mishap before too much time passes. In my situation, my back was turned, and until I smelled it, I had no idea that powdery joint compound was recoating the walls, floor and countertops behind me.

During the project, neighbors and friends often dropped by to offer consultation, commentary and flat-out help. Without my asking, one friend volunteered to spray-texture the walls. She explained it was her way of paying forward some of the contributions she wanted to make in life. Her kindness touched us. But I was elated for other reasons, too. First, this would camouflage my plaster goofs. Second, I'd learn by doing when my turn came to give spray-texturing a try.

However, as I observed her artistry, I knew to stay out of it. My participation would have been akin to grabbing the brush from O'Keeffe, yelling "cut" on the set of a Scorsese film or adding a kazoo to Bach's Cello Suites.

In some cultures, weavers who handcraft exquisite Persian rugs purposely slip in one imperceptible imperfection. Their reasoning is that only God can be perfect and they do not want to challenge the All-Mighty. In so many ways, I'm with them. Our kitchen project was my Persian rug and I was no threat to the throne. I left behind a hundred reasons for the Creator to rest comfortably.

Around the House

The Look of Laughter

We had a family husky named Lupin. She had that knockout Northern look, kind of like a scaled-down wolf. Glam-shots aside, I'd never met a soul so full of life coupled with an irritating sense of humor. The dog put me in the aisles sometimes… Sometimes.

I tried skijoring with Lupin even though I'm not good on skis. Gravity has its way with me. I've played a fair amount of hockey, but skate blades are considerably shorter than skis. With skating, my natural reaction to imbalance is to step one foot over the other. I found I can't do that with skis. Hence, I topple. Lupin thought this was quite a giggle. To her credit, she'd come back to me to check on my welfare, then lick me like a hunk of carrion.

On another skijoring attempt, she schemed her version of crack the whip. She and I had gathered some steam along the trail and I began feeling genuine Nordic success. Then she inexplicably stopped and sat down. Braking isn't my forte either. I whizzed by, grabbing at any branch available to slow myself down. Lupin's head turned, following my course of travel to watch where I ended up down trail.

For the record, I'm not a musher either. But DyAnne and I are big mushing fans. We had a kicksled for Lupin made of old hockey sticks, cross-country skis and hockey tape. Ironically, this miniature sled was for her exercise, but I'm the one who got the workout.

Either Dy or I acted as the carrot for Lupin to chase, and the other rode on the sled runners or pedaled with one leg off to the side. One below-zero day, we took Lupin out and broke trail in knee-deep snow. Minutes later, I began shedding layers of clothing as sweat dripped from my eyebrows onto the inside of my glasses. While I gulped air, Lupin simply glanced at me over her shoulder, still breathing through her nose.

A friend took me mushing for my first time on a full-size sled with huskies who do it for a living. I received three dogs and some coaching. Rule number one: never, ever, ever let go of the sled or I might not see those dogs and that sled again for miles.

I pulled the sled's snow hook from the ground, the gangline snapped tight and those dogs opened all engines instantly. We top-ended in just a few strides and rounded the first bend smoothly. But two turns later, I abandoned the hang-on advice. The team veered right and an ill-placed mogul bounced me to the left. After an airborne moment, I plunged face-first into a snowbank.

Hilarity is an odd thing. I've seen it on Lupin's face and recognized that same look in the dog team. It's what stopped them in their tracks. So I got back on the runners that threw me. Even I had to admit, the facial imprint I left in the snow looked a lot like me.

Lupin was one dog. I can only imagine the power of running twelve or fourteen or sixteen all at once. I can't help but wonder how she would have stacked up on a sled team, the kind of runner she'd have been: lead dog, wheel dog or somewhere in-between. But as for kennel leadership, she was a soul to ignite kindred frivolity and everyone would have stayed on top of their game.

Garden Grunt

There's a certain pleasure in being grunt labor for a garden. For one, it doesn't involve much thinking. DyAnne is the gardener in our family and she works out the math behind the plants. Occasionally, I'll throw in a suggestion about fertilizer. I'd like to think I'm somewhat versed in piling it higher and deeper.

For another, I get to mess with power tools and play in the dirt. We got a new tiller that required assembly. I'm an instruction follower, but I don't know why. The manuals I come across usually leave out key directions and put the brakes on a project. So I wing it, which typically calls for minimal thought. But with this tiller, the instructions flowed without a hitch from Step 1 through Step 36, Subsection 4B. I initially installed the handle upside down but recognized the error in time to make corrections before the situation spun out of control. As such, I've got a good feeling about this tiller. We haven't started it yet, but I'm confident. The instructions recommended waiting on starting until closer to tilling time. That way the gas doesn't sit too long and go stale. If it's in the instructions, I'm willing to try it at least once.

Mother's Day is our annual trip to area greenhouses for starter plants. In northern Minnesota, we're in plant-hardiness Zone 3. A rough rule of thumb around these parts is to purchase plants on Mother's Day, but don't be surprised if they're not safely in the ground until Father's Day.

My responsibilities at the greenhouse are to negotiate one of their rusty shopping carts that's customized for plant transport through narrow, bumpy aisles. Sometimes Dy puts me in charge of procuring tomatoes because I can identify those without much help. Again, not a lot of thought there. I'm pleased with my growth since last year at recognizing some of our favorite herbs. I'm spot on with rosemary, not too bad at basil, but thyme can throw me on occasion. Most ornamental plants are out of my league. I make valiant guesses anyway.

Hanging out with the shopping cart is also a good place to people-watch. I see other grunts like myself down the rows doing the same thing. There's something in our eyes when we lock on to each other's gaze. It silently speaks to the importance of our role. It's good work if you can get it.

My greatest pleasure is simply observing Dy meticulously selecting plants. She examines them for bugs, checks for color and calculates how best to ensure their survival until planting. It's spiritual for her. She's learned well from that quiet Beatle who was actually a gardener in disguise. George Harrison never claimed that the soil and plant life were his. He just tended to them. The garden belongs to a larger entity.

Gardening for Dy is similar to hunting for me. If we're lucky, harvest from the garden and harvest from the forest will team up on our dinner table.

The Evolution of Priorities

My first car was a low-riding, muffler-dragging behemoth that was tailormade for my grandfather. The 1972 Chevy Caprice, the largest sedan Chevy had ever manufactured, was just what he ordered. When he decided to hang up his keys, it became mine for the taking. I painted it primer grey and named it the Land Shark.

Having developed my highway skills inside a snug Volkswagen Beetle, the Land Shark was a different beast. It seemed to sprawl across a lane and a half. The hood was long enough to seat a congressional hearing. The trunk was so cavernous that reaching for the tire iron was nothing short of falling down basement steps.

Mechanically, pulling into traffic was gulp-worthy. The accelerator stuck, hesitated to send fuel to the motor and getting up to speed required multiple hiccups from under the hood. Checking the Shark's gas mileage was impossible. A hole had rusted through the top of the fuel tank and filling it with gas was futile. But what I didn't know didn't hurt me. The gas gauge needle moved faster than the speedometer needle anyway. I didn't care. It was my first set of wheels and I no longer had to borrow the keys.

Inheriting the car also precluded learning to haggle with a seller. For better or worse, I've found that inconsequential. I bond with vehicles and keep them for as long as they run safely. For me, purchases occur only once every couple of decades. So from cost to gizmos, I don't always know what to expect in newer models.

The lists of so-called "improvements" on factory fresh vehicles seem endless and useless. I don't see how power cup holders, reclining clocks and hi-def, surround-sound GPS screens will make me feel safer or more luxurious. But they are enough to ignite the sticker like a Molotov cocktail right there in the showroom.

After 21 years, our Chevy Blazer called it a career. The new pony in our driveway is a 2014, pre-driven, Chevy Silverado, shiny black and really sweet. DyAnne and I aren't whistles and bells kind of people. But even the basic work-truck version of this Silverado came with a few extras and I've had to adjust.

I don't see the point in keyless remote entries. I'm good with walking up to the door; it's a requirement for getting in. But nowadays, there's only one keyhole for all four doors and those key fobs are so bulky I might as well carry a shot put in my pocket.

I'm not big on heated seats. They make me feel like I'm sitting in a puddle of warm something. This is northern Minnesota and long johns protect me just fine from the coldest interior cab upholstery.

Ironically, I figured a CD player was an automatic extra. Silly assumption. Turns out technology has evolved and CDs are going the way of the eight-track. I still have tower upon CD tower of those essential road buddies. So I bought a CD boombox to ride shotgun.

The Silverado is bigger than the Blazer, too. For me, it's not a macho thing and getting used to its size is proof. I tried parallel parking it near a downtown curb. "Near" is the operative phrase here, but "vicinity" might be more accurate. The truck was closer to the fenders of oncoming traffic than it was the sidewalk.

Determined to rectify such ineptitude, I drove around the block and the same parking spot was still open. As I backed in, I knew I was close to the curb when I felt some resistance against the rear tire. After a quick straighten-out and feeling satisfied, I got out and looked. The tire had jumped the gutter and onto the sidewalk. I left it there…went into the store like that was my intent all along.

As for backing up a boat trailer, I could thread a needle with that Blazer. But the Silverado hides our small trailer completely from sight either in the side mirrors or by looking directly out the back window. By the time the trailer comes into view, swerving has begun and we serpentine down the landing, a little something for onlooker entertainment.

With some practice, I figure the Silverado and I will come to terms. Two decades from now, after we've snooped down logging roads and it's clawed me through bumper-deep snow, when maybe it's time to get another, we'll have lived a lot of life together. Its sentimental value will have risen to the status of family member—just like the Blazer.

Be Careful with Your Carcass

Holiday trimmings aren't just décor at our house. In keeping with holiday spirit, we also share food trimmings with our neighborhood ravens. Offering the bones of animals who gave themselves to us is the least we can do. Nothing goes unappreciated.

When the holidays roll around, we want to make sure the ravens have a bountiful season. Over the years, we've had lessons in learning how to distribute leftovers properly without annoying our neighbors. Ravens are an avian road crew. They clean up everything from roadkill to milkshakes. Trouble is, ravens have a whole different set of table manners than we do. There's more to it than serving from the left and clearing from the right.

Our culinary extras draw ravens close to our house, allowing us to observe their behavior. They're fascinating to watch, strutting and attired like they're attending a black-tie affair. At times, the satin sheen of sunshine on their midnight feathers is so bright it colors them white.

We became versed in raven etiquette after our first Thanksgiving at the house where we live now. Having trimmed final leftovers from the turkey, we decided against boiling the bones for soup and opted to set the carcass in the backyard for the ravens. Herein lie lessons number one through three: Ravens are deceptively strong. They don't wait to be asked. And they love carryout.

No sooner had I returned inside the house, than I glanced back at my delivery. The turkey carcass was missing. After a quick search, I found it on our neighbor's garage roof. For a moment it was unattended, then a raven landed beside it and began feasting.

Word evidently spread quickly through the raven community and moments later, as holidays will go, relatives came swooping in.

Fortunately for neighborly relations, the carcass had dropped onto the slope of the roof opposite their house. From inside, our neighbors couldn't see the commotion on the other side of the garage ridgeline.

Ravens don't monkey around with comestible opportunities. Not a morsel remained on that turkey skeleton. When they finished, I bussed the garage roof…servings from our leftovers, cleared away with our rake.

A Dog, a Birch, a Birdsong

I made the appointment with the veterinary clinic, then turned off my cellphone. After months of struggling to make the right decision, reality sank in and nausea overwhelmed me. Our husky Lupin and I had twenty minutes left in our life together.

It was a home visit and Dr. Chip stepped into our kitchen. Lupin had always taken a shine to Chip. As soon as she saw him, she plastered her ears back and went all a'shiver. It was an up day for her. But in just a glance, Chip nodded his head and reaffirmed our observations. It was time.

He gave her the sedative and the four of us walked to our backyard. We put her blanket in the shade of the birch by her kennel where she often played or supervised the neighborhood. She laid down and nodded off.

I expected the second injection, the one that sent her over, to take instant effect. But Chip had to administer three doses of the drug. We could see her breathe occasionally. Dy and I continued to give her scratches on the areas of her body she most requested. I don't know how conscious Lupin was of it or of our talking. Because I had some questions.

Lupin had suffered enough. Her illness, whatever it was that even specialists couldn't determine, had become a year of extensive tests and eliminations that showed what it wasn't. Diagnostics had been exhausted. Dr. Chip's best estimate was a circulation cancer like lymphoma or leukemia.

I asked why she wasn't passing. Apparently, the sedation shot significantly drops blood pressure. However, that makes hitting a vein directly for the lethal injection more challenging. Fortunately, the sedative made Lupin completely unaware of what was happening. Scientifically, that sounded reasonable and I wanted to believe it. But I wasn't emotionally convinced.

Not knowing is cold-blooded helplessness. I could have more easily lived had Lupin decided to depart on her own. We'd have dealt with her absence and at least been spared the additional agony of us determining when she'd die. If the decision were ours, I'd have loved being handed a distinct answer, to have that work done for me so her pain wouldn't string out. But that's just selfishness on my part. Higher powers don't swoop in and get us off the hook. I had to put in the work that life was asking of me.

Chip and I carried Lupin's body in her blanket to the bed of his pickup. We would get her ashes back. Oddly, throughout this ordeal, I realized a bird had been singing right above us. I didn't see it and didn't recognize its song. But it had a bubbling, flute-like melody. When Chip drove away, I looked for the bird, but the song had stopped. Dy told me later that she'd heard it, too.

Lupin's disease started when she was nine and woke up with a closed left eye. Only the week before, she had received an outstanding checkup at her annual visit to the clinic. She had remissions during her illness, but over time we knew her condition was declining severely. She was off her dish, turned down favorites like peas and carrots, and wasn't sneaking up behind me to snitch the last of my banana. Dy eventually handfed her anything she'd ingest just to get some kind of nutrition in her. She ate so slowly we thought maybe her mouth was sore.

But her personality was waning, resting or hiding, too. Sometimes it felt as if she had already left us. She was coping with whatever was wrong and we weren't going to begrudge her a thing. The night before she died, we let her sleep on the bed with us.

On her day of passing, Lupin's high spirits like her old self only compounded the decision to euthanize her. However, Dr. Chip offered us the most insightful advice I'd ever received to make that dreadful decision. He brought science and emotion at least somewhat closer for me.

He told us this was the window of time we wanted for her. Our hearts want to hang on. But we had to look at the slope of her condition and ask, what are we going to make her go through? "If someone knows their pet won't live until spring, why put them through a dark, cold winter?" he analogized. Her comfort was primary during this window and it had a single criterion: If the decision to euthanize was unmistakably clear, then we had waited too long.

We wanted to keep her passing moment private and close to home. We'd let neighbors and friends know in due time. But word spread without us uttering a peep. For sixteen years and counting, our neighbors have known each others' dogs by name, living or deceased. Each neighbor frequently checked on Lupin's welfare. After she left us, they came to our rescue in their own way. And not all of them were human.

The two women who lived across the back alley brought us a bouquet of flowers they had handpicked from their garden. When the guy across the side street saw Dy walking alone in the alley behind his house, he inquired about Lupin's absence. Dy explained, and as she turned to continue her walk, he gave her the Catholic sign of the cross. The deep importance of his beliefs conferred ineffable blessings to us.

Lupin's descent also occurred during the peak of COVID. As a result, the veterinary clinic had cut back drastically on home visits. But they made an exception for Lupin. Dr. Chip, Dy and I were with her in the backyard talking through our protective masks. As we waited, Chip mentioned some personal feelings that most vets can't help but have. They treat patients who they uniquely care about. When those animals pass, their departure is emotionally difficult for the doctors. One of those dogs was Lupin, a husky who made the clinic staff smile and who didn't flinch during a blood draw.

Not long after her passing, a tree service crew showed up at our house and my nausea returned. We had consulted them about the longevity of the birch tree. It was weak and ragged. The likelihood of it surviving winter was slim. If we waited too long, it would surely fall and damage our garage. In just a few hours, its branches that had provided shade in summer, color in fall and places for birds to perch would no longer be part of our lives.

But the crew disassembled it with such dignity that my queasiness subsided. The strategy for each cut was performed with fascinating perception. They had no cherry-picker. Instead, they harnessed a lacework of ropes and pulleys among the branches for a cutter to ascend the tree and not fall out. Trunk pieces and large branches were lowered to the ground one at a time rather than sent unceremoniously crashing down. When nearly finished, the cutter stood towering above the uppermost tip of the trunk with nothing but the climbing spikes around his calves holding him on. The operation was so impressive, neighbors gathered to watch.

Only twenty feet of the trunk remained. There was a gaping void in the backyard where the birch used to be. So much visible sky. So much new to see. But just before the final cuts were made, a small bird returned to the birch and joined the cutter in the tree. The bird clung to the one remaining twig sticking out of the bark. It chirped a few notes. It was the same song we had heard from above Lupin when she crossed over.

One of the women who brought us the flowers was standing nearby and heard it. Dy mentioned the bird's song when Lupin passed, and how we were unsettled with the three injections and length of time it took.

Our neighbor and friend leaned in gently, "She wanted to hear the end of the song."

From Husky to House Dog

She was born with gifted intelligence not so much in a bookworm way, but more of a Hannibal Lecter way—she can peer into my soul and know she's got me cornered. It's helping shape me as her dad.

Her name is Mustang Sally and by definition she's an Alaskan husky, a working dog. Through centuries of DNA, she was designed by nature to pull. It's an attribute not always conducive to transforming a husky into a house dog. But her work includes a side hustle. It's to work me over, especially my nerves.

Sally was the runt of her litter, as if her mother had just enough cookie dough to squeeze out one more small one. Like all Alaskan huskies, she's not a purebred. However, she is of Iditarod royalty and heiress to that gene pool. Her great-grandfather was an Iditarod champion in 2011. That might sound like lineage bragging rights, but as canines go, it's too much horsepower just to pull a kick sled and walk on a leash.

Her cunning operates in a multitude of ways. DyAnne and I have tried training her through positive reinforcement. We give her small treats when she responds admirably to our instruction, such as urinating outdoors. When she's off kilter, we use those treats to redirect her from whatever is leading her astray, such as a pair of moccasins begging to be snitched. However, she's quickly discerned ways to increase her profit margin. For instance, peeing multiple times in short spurts garners more snacks than a singular, extended one. She'll also knowingly misbehave, then sit beside me as if to say, "After those monkeyshines, I guess I'll need some more of that positive reinforcement."

Her physical toughness became apparent the first time she counter-surfed for food and swiped a jalapeno pepper. Far from concerned, I welcomed this educational opportunity. The pepper was my accomplice in the classroom; it would do the teaching. Sally strutted from the kitchen with her jalapeno treasure. But when she returned smacking her lips looking for more, I realized there was no defense against this rapid-fire gremlin.

With a mouth like a musky, her puppy teeth have penetrated the sturdiest Carhartt clothing. But her preference is to nip unprotected soft spots on arms and legs. She and I also had a collision that she won. Running wide open, her small forty-one-pound frame took me out at the knees and flipped me ankles over armpits. She trotted away unscathed. I had broken ribs, a cracked wrist and a lump the size of a golf ball protruding from my skull.

Disciplinary tussles are fruitless and light skirmishes mount into brawls. To her, that's playtime. If she were a farm dog, she'd be one to chase down vehicles driving along the dirt road. She also scolds anything that's out of place even if it's inanimate, like water buckets, waste baskets and brooms. She bites at water from the garden hose and once managed to wrangle the hose from my hand. The hose handle bounced on the ground, fired a stream and shot me up the ass. There's no looking dignified in the neighborhood under those circumstances.

Unfortunately, neighbors are part of the problem. They think she's adorable. Try living with it folks. I'll say this much, I'm realizing it takes a neighborhood to raise a husky. We now have a waiting list for those who want to take her skijoring.

Making light of her hijinks humors me through my feeble quest for compromise. But I've begun noticing her root-beer brown eyes. Sometimes they're disguised in her black fur or she's too occupied to give me a sideways glance. Lately though, I've detected expression when we look each other in the eyes and I think it's helped settle some of the dust between us. Maybe I'm *not* an incapable dad.

When I've gone to Major League Baseball games, I can't help but observe parents and their children. I see those kids wearing shiny, new batting helmets, gulping hot dogs and dripping ice cream. I consider what led up to that and what makes the moment special for them all. But I'm also aware of the cost for goodies and souvenirs at major league venues. I think about parents who can't afford to take their kids to those events. I wonder how they overcome heartbreak and respond when their child asks to go.

Mustang Sally is still young and I hope my story with her is long from over. She and I walked to her kennel the other day and I disconnected her leash once we were inside. Then, as is our custom, I stepped out, closed the gate and she sat waiting for me to pull a treat from what she figures is my Magic Pocket. But as I did, I fumbled its transfer to her mouth and the treat fell into the snow. I dug around but couldn't find it again. It was the last one I had.

She stared at the place where it disappeared, then looked back at my pocket. Her eyes asked me to keep trying. As if I could take her to a major league ballgame someday.

Memoirs from a Couch

Detailed woodwork and intricate craftsmanship are signatures of heirloom furniture. I think of antique dressers, designer headboards and ornate dining tables.

I don't think of couches. They aren't like that. They wear out. Rare is the beloved couch that's been handed down for generations. Once they go south, there's no return short of spendy restoration. If they're passed along at all, they might find themselves in a college frat house.

DyAnne and I have needed a new couch for about a decade. Since acknowledging that problem, my support group tells me I'm halfway there. But a course of action is more complex. I struggle with when we should actually commit to the investment. Reasons crop up in favor of waiting a little longer.

Three years ago, we eked more mileage out of our old couch when a puppy came into our lives. She's our husky, Mustang Sally. I just didn't see the point in getting a new couch when the old one serves well as an oversized chew toy. Sally wasted no time in rounding off its edges and corners like the buzzsaw she is. But for that couch, it really doesn't matter anymore. As long as she doesn't choke on the stuffing, what the hell.

I'm trying to look at the hard facts. The couch has thrown support rods. The springs sing arias when the sofa bed folds out. The mattress is colored with splotches and unknown beverage spills have rusted the frame. The cushions cave in the middle and we sit lower than on the seat of a chopped-out Harley-Davidson. I have the advantage of being taller than DyAnne, which is why I get the saggiest side of the couch. But I don't begrudge her that luxury. When we sit on the couch to eat and watch videos, she's at chin-level with the dinner plate on the table in front of her.

Standing up from the couch is like extraction from a beanbag chair. Unfortunately, the couch is no longer beanbag-comfortable. Naps on it are more active exercise than restful slumber. Neck and back muscles go into lockdown if we sit too long. Mobility thereafter requires foot stomps to recirculate blood.

Then there's the whole stigma of what the neighbors will think. One night we invited the guy from across the street over and he picked the couch as a place to sit. During dinner, he dug one knee into the wooden floor like a kickstand to hold himself in place. No one has come to dinner since.

Considering its years of loyalty, I can't badmouth the old couch. We have backstories more numerous than the peanuts that have fallen between the cushions. The couch and television team up as the entertainment hub of our home. From that couch, we've witnessed miraculous feats of athleticism by sports heroes who are now in their respective halls of fame. Classic TV programs date back to the original run of *Northern Exposure* and *CBS Sunday Morning* when Charles Kuralt was the first host. VHS, DVD and YouTube technology came along years afterward and now allow us to relive those programs—on that same couch—whenever we want.

The old couch also cradled us during difficult phone calls. We sat on that couch with our cats at the moment each passed over to the other side. And we lived through the tragedies of breaking news on television. We couldn't pry ourselves off the couch throughout that gut-wrenching day in September 2001.

For several years, our three nieces have come to our house for long weekends of exuberant catch-up and laughter. While here, they sit side-by-side on the old couch like the Culhanes from the vintage TV show *Hee Haw*. Yet, they've never uttered so much as a whimper about discomfort. The niece in the middle sags the most. But at least it's a balanced sag. The nieces on the ends angle inward, then counter for it by leaning on the armrests.

During one winter visit, we took a hike to see some ingenuity on the Northern landscape. Local snow carvers often adorn area lakes with snow furniture. Thanks to their creativity, we enjoyed snow thrones, snow televisions, snow barbecue grills, snow beds, snow bars and snow appliances. No need to retrieve the beverages we brought from the snow fridge; the couch chilled them for us.

As we left, I joked that the snow couch was probably more comfy than the one back at our house. They were silent.

Maybe it was time for a new couch.

Three years later, I agreed. Our new couch just arrived. It's good, but temporary. Mustang Sally is young and we're still trying to curtail her chewing addiction. Our plan is to buy another, better couch once she matures. We estimate that'll happen when she's a kennel elder.

However, the addition of the new couch left us no room for the old one. The time had come to part. I hate dumping in the landfill. The old couch won't be used for parts. It won't be recycled into anything. But plopping it in the front yard for someone else to take to *their* home for "free" just didn't sit right with me.

Our neighbor and I maneuvered the old couch out the living room door to our pickup. It was like carrying a stretcher. We slid it onto the bed. The next day, Dy and I drove it to the transfer station and pushed it over the railing into the dumpster below. I didn't watch it drop.

Youth Undergrowth

Funding the Future

A defensive lineman came knocking at the door. He asked for money. So I gave him some.

This enterprising young man introduced himself as an eighth-grade member of the Timberwolves high school football team. He explained they needed a new scoreboard and were seeking donations. From his strapping demeanor, I quickly surmised they've scored so many points over the years that they burned out the last of their lightbulbs.

I liked the cut of his jib. He had gone to practice at 7:30 that morning, spent three hours of grunt-and-groan, and here he was in late afternoon pounding the pavement for the team. He also delivers our weekly Shopper.

Door-to-door sales can be a rough gig for a kid. I remember a hockey dad from my peewee days who masterminded a fundraiser for us little players to sell a truckload of plastic toothpick dispensers he'd come across. Now there's a commodity that'd upend Wall Street. The dispenser looked like a miniature rocket ship on a base. In theory, pressing down on the contraption's spring-loaded cone would force a small rod upward and push a toothpick out from inside. In reality, its success ratio was about one in every ten. It cost seven cents wholesale and was going for two bucks retail. And we were supposed to make money off those things.

Today's youth fundraisers seem to have become more sophisticated and creative. They go beyond raffles that no one ever wins and Halloween candy that everyone gives away. Donors these days get more for their money. The soft canvas grocery bags from the high school trap shooting team are sturdy enough to carry canned food or a half-dozen sleeves of clay pigeons. The scoreboard donation included discounts at area restaurants and merchants who we actually frequent. Throughout the years, we've also had some delightful cheese and sausage platters. However, I do confess that the quality of fundraiser pizzas can vary. We've found that some have more flavor if the cardboard tray is eaten intact.

Therefore, I asked for more information about my investment before committing to the scoreboard. My guy's description left me gobsmacked. Based on funds raised, they could "optimize the board to enhance spectator experience." It was nothing short of a Jumbotron.

I discovered that lightbulbs have gone the way of leather helmets. They've been replaced with high-tech, ten-millimeter, pixel-pitch LEDs. Video capabilities include: players saluting the crowd during pre-game roster introductions; replays of bonehead officiating; and a Kiss-Cam that captures images of real-time activities below the bleachers. Even fans standing in line at the concession would be able to keep up with on-field action through satellite screens positioned above the stand. All of this just to tally the score and track the time.

Since I can remember, my donation policy has been based on my budget—first come, first donated. If someone stops by with a later request for the same purpose, I regretfully have to decline. Girl Scout cookies can be the one exception. I'll dip into grocery funds and scour under truck mats for loose change to go the extra box that'll feed my addiction.

I like when kids participate directly in the fundraising because it reaches beyond financial gain for their cause. Point systems are sometimes established to offer kids motivation for top sales, or tiered incentives allow them to sell at whatever level they can achieve. Direct participation is also filled with indirect life-lessons. It teaches kids goal-setting, the value of rejection and how to articulate a spoken presentation that doesn't sound like they've got a sled dog bootie Velcroed to their tongue.

A fifth-grade girl came to our house with the same card of coupons as the defensive lineman. I assumed she was helping the scoreboard effort. But she presented a couple of twists that my donation policy didn't account for. She was raising funds for a class field trip to an environmental center. So while the donor benefits were identical, the cause was different.

She filled me in about the trip and her educational interests. In getting to know her, I asked where she lived within the school district. "I live over in…" she began, then her voice double-clutched. After the hesitation, she blurted the name of the low-rent housing complex, followed with a quick, "But we're moving into a house next month."

Especially in a small town, kids have to rely on the same contributors rather than cultivating new markets. I've begun reassessing my donation policy.

The Elements of Hooey

The group of nine—parents, siblings, cousins, aunties and uncles—endured the arduous twelve-hour drive to Ely Outfitting Company in northern Minnesota. But the anticipation of backcountry canoeing and camping fueled their resolve. With unshackled enthusiasm, they unpacked, then repacked their gear to prepare for a week of paddling. The eleven-year-old twin brothers were particularly incapable of containing their fever to get on-trail. Finally, everyone clustered beside their Chevy Suburban and the wilderness shuttle van that would transport them to the entry point of Heaven. I introduced myself as their shuttle driver.

The plan was for them to first follow me in their Suburban to the end point of the trip. From there, they'd park, then pile into the shuttle for the remaining drive to their entry point. Usually, I'm alone in the shuttle during that first leg of travel. But for this group, the twins' mother asked if I'd mind the two brothers riding with me from the start.

When I most certainly agreed, a wild-west stampede commenced to the passenger side of the shuttle. Their furor was surpassed only when I asked, "Who's riding shotgun?" The brothers scrapped and shoved each other until one of them plunked into the passenger seat.

Their names were Jason and Jeremy. And though they were only eleven, they touted just as many years of wilderness experience. What's more, their status as twins featured a twist—their birthdays were four days apart. I'd like to think I'm somewhat skilled in knowing hooey when I hear it, so I found all this questionable—*They'd scramble to ride shotgun, but not clamber over each other to be first into the world?* I decided to research that later or check with their mom at the entry point.

Jason won the shotgun seat, but Jeremy took full advantage of the entire back for himself. He began voicing plans to renovate the interior: tear out the seats behind the driver and install a table, then turn the rear seats lengthwise for camper-style bedding.

With those amenities in place, our conversation turned to wildlife. When they found I deer hunt, they asked questions about deer behavior in the north woods. As we talked, three deer bolted from a ditch and I slammed the brakes to miss them. "That would be *bad* deer behavior," I said. The two laughed, so at least I earned some giggle points.

In light of their extensive camping background, they explained textbook precautions their family takes to keep bears from entering camp. They hang their food pack at least twelve feet off the ground and six feet from the tree trunk.

As if mentioning food triggered it, a fifty-pound shadow crossed ahead of us and lumbered into the woods. I slowed for a look when we reached the spot. Just inside the forest fringe, a black bear cub posed, hind legs on the ground, front paws against a tree, ready to claw upward. Mother Nature was cooperating nicely.

"Every time we talk about an animal, we see one," Jason said. "So now let's talk about moose."

We didn't have a lot more exclusive time together, but I couldn't believe our luck again. The gravel road we were on had been freshly graded. The shoulder grit was moist, dark and unblemished—except for a single trail. Hoofprints the length of a football trekked alongside of us for a hundred yards before returning to the forest. A moose had come onto the road not long before. Though we never saw the moose attached to the tracks, it made an impression.

"Now let's talk about unicorns," Jeremy said, and we all laughed.

"Then let's talk about Sasquatch," Jason countered, producing more chortles.

But that one I could accommodate. Here was my turn to test their twaddle meter and the timing was magic.

I started with a story that's actually true. "Funny you should mention," I said. "Whether for real or just to party, a group of Bigfoot fans sometimes search for it at a lake just north of your entry point."

We approached a road sign tacked to a tree. As we got closer, I said, "Do me a favor and tell me what that sign says on the tree up there. I need to know if it's changed." They could see the word "DANGER" pre-printed in red across the top. But in the white space below it, they saw the handwritten words, "Bigfoot Crossing."

They blurted appropriate bewilderment for just a moment, then Jason collected himself. "Did you put that there?"

Nothing got by these guys…And no, I didn't put it there.

Their eleven years of wilderness training became clear at the entry point. The family evacuated the shuttle. Nobody spoke except Dad who uttered just one reminder, "No one goes anywhere without carrying something." With the efficiency of Navy Seals, they had two canoes off the trailer before I even had one untied. I never did get to ask Mom about the twins' birthdays. She was already down-trail shouldering a Duluth pack and carrying paddles.

Riding alone back to town, I stopped for another look at the Bigfoot sign. It had been there about three years and the handwritten lettering was fading. So I returned to my house and did some homework.

First, I found that twins actually can be born days or even months apart. I also came across the Bigfoot Field Researchers Organization website and it dispelled some misconceptions. The organization is hardly a group of Bigfoot pranksters passing the bottle around the campfire. Their mission is to legitimately resolve the Bigfoot mystery through conclusive documentation that the species exists. This includes investigating and rating the credibility of human encounters. Some of those accounts in northern Minnesota have taken place at locations I know, like my deer hunting area and that lake north of Jason and Jeremy's entry point.

A few months later, I went back to the Bigfoot Crossing sign. I don't know exactly why, but I took a Sharpie marker with me and re-darkened the lines of the handwritten lettering.

21st Century Pictographs

Eight people stood on a wilderness overlook with their backs to the pristine lake below. Not one of them held a camera. They were seemingly oblivious to the glorious panorama behind them. Instead, they gazed at renderings on a sheer cliff directly beside the gravel road opposite the lake. "My God," they were agape, "Who'd have thought?"

That "thought" likely had little to do with interpretations of ancient pictographs found in these parts. This group stood before a wall of doodlings and text that flat-out defaces Mother Nature. Though graffiti artists might disagree, it's a visual oxymoron to the surrounding unblemished magnificence. As appeasement, I try to appreciate this blasphemy as twenty-first century pictographs. Their expressive content just deciphers more simply than their timeworn counterparts. Plus, today's paint doesn't last as long.

Captivated that such artwork ventured beyond metropolitan architecture, the group absorbed this tableau as if Moses had delivered it personally. They mused on the logo for "Matt's Racing & Auto Body" and appeared smitten with Will's proclamations of love for Alice. If vandalism were charged, that one wouldn't be hard to track down. But seven years later, Will and Alice's relationship faded like the spray-can paint that announced it and was covered by something more current.

I'm not big on defiling Mother Nature's art gallery. But I can't be entirely huffy. For years, I've spent time pondering these very graphics. The cliff stretches about a tenth of a mile and quite honestly, it's full of upbeat stuff. There are the most complimentary thoughts on God. And according to the writing on the wall, "Jesus Saves…

Coupons." The coupons part looked to have been added later because the handwriting is different.

Colorful peace symbols are abundant. Amateur attempts at intimidation like "Who you lookin' at?" are countered with "Love & Smiles." One tastefully done nude is reminiscent of Picasso's Blue Period, a stroke of genius from the up-and-coming artist who probably worked with Rust-Oleum.

I must say, considering all that artistic canvas, there's barely a cuss word on it. I've given my life to language and it's meant to be used. So unless I misunderstand some shrouded treachery in the meanings, the rare four-letter words on the cliffside are pretty mild vernacular. I admit, however, that I'm disappointed in the only use of the f-bomb. Normally, it's one of my favorites. But this falls flat. It just hangs like a dangling participle, ineffective, as if the writer did it just to say they tagged a dirty word on public property and nothing more. What a waste. What's its point?

Such is the nature of pictographs. They have everybody guessing. There's a well-preserved site of genuine pictographs not far from the graffiti wall. It's a three-mile drive back down the road, then a two-mile canoe paddle or snowshoe to a lake northward. The old pictographs are somewhat smaller compared to the roadside visuals that ambush travelers passing by the cliff. Without paying attention, visitors could overlook the ancient paintings.

Having lived in the region for approximately nine-thousand years, the Ojibwe people are considered the likely creators of this artwork. The estimated age of these pictographs is five-hundred to one-thousand years old. The immortal paint is understood to be a mix of iron hematite, boiled sturgeon spine and bear grease.

Some of the depictions are obvious: a bull moose, a human, a canine or maybe a cat, and presumably some canoes. Beyond that, only mysteries remain. Scholars hypothesize that they represent Ojibwe traditions, legends and spirituality. Others speculate that some pictographs are connected to constellations typically seen in winter. The human among the pictographs has been interpreted as Orion. Thus, the celestial representations could be a celebration of the hunting and storytelling season. Some people have suggested the drawings possibly served as navigational directions toward hunting grounds. An ice-covered lake would also have provided better access and firmer footing than open water for the artist while working on the project.

Then again, perhaps the pictographs are an early indicator of offbeat humor. Throughout history, humankind has been populated by the exceptionally playful. On the day, week, or whenever these pictographs were created, maybe the artist was feeling a little mischievous. Weary of mapping redundant images from one cliffside to the next, perhaps this painter was an avant-garde of the time, itching to explore, break a few rules, go deeper for art, conjure laughter. That might explain why Orion's image portrays him with disproportionately long arms stretched far out to either side, as if exaggerating the abundance of moose or lying about the length of a fish. It exhibits a common bond of creative minds across the centuries. Orion is telling a whopper.

Act Your Age

So I was in a bar. Billy's to be exact. It's a warm, welcoming, family kind of place in the country. At the time, it was also the finish line for the John Beargrease Sled Dog Marathon. Billy's features outstanding food and servers almost as fun as a young man I met.

The final dog team had come in and Billy's was packed with mushers, handlers, race officials, volunteers, and fans like DyAnne and me. Kids were abundant.

A musher, face awash from four days on-trail, was paying his bill at the bar while his two boys waited politely behind him. They were an arm's length from our standup table and I saw that the nine-year-old was wearing a Minnesota Vikings hat. Being the Green Bay Packers fan I am, and in a bloody-Mary mood, I wasn't about to let the moment slip by. I called his attention to my Packers hat.

That was all it took. This seemingly placid fella instantly uploaded a glut of Packers mockery. The next thing I knew, I time-traveled back to fourth-grade and went toe-to-toe with this modern-day rascal, each of us unleashing derisive jokes about the other guy's team.

I soon realized I was at a disadvantage. Every weekday, he's on the pulse of opposing-team indignities by mere virtue of having elementary school classmates. As a freelance writer, I'm an office of one. I have no water cooler down the hallway to cavort with co-workers on the latest pop jabs and taunts. Skol Boy rebuffed my ancient quips about the Vikings' reputation as chokers, then retorted with something about my Packers hat and a pooper-scooper.

I had to somehow slide out of our exchange without him knowing I have no water cooler.

Quite honestly, he had me laughing so hard I didn't think of my top-shelf comebacks anyway. So I gave him a high-five and he understood our semantic gun-slinging was all in good fun.

But as he and his family left Billy's, he was determined to have the final zinger. He stopped next to a corner pocket of the pool table and looked back at me. He lifted his boot, sniffed the sole and somewhere through the muddling of bar noise I heard him say the word "Packers" but nothing else. His body language spoke the rest.

Close to True

Cooking Up Fish Tales

Four-foot waves hurled the defenseless canoes about like empty Styrofoam coolers. Torrential rain erased the paddlers from each other's sight. The cacophony of breakers pile-driving a jagged shoreline drowned out the group's impotent cries for mercy.

But a man among men in the lead canoe had a 41-inch northern pike thrashing...

No, let's make that 44…

Okay... *a 44-inch northern pike thrashing to the Ballet of Mythical Beasts across the whitecaps. His ultralight tackle withstood no more, disintegrating 'neath the strain. Devoid of conscious thought, the man plunged overboard, wrestled the fish into a bear hug and heaved it into the hull. Back aboard, he deftly took its measurements. And the fish—caught and released for another angler another day—apparated safely into the ancient depths of its home.*

A big story. I like it because it isn't mine. But I was there when it came to life.

From spring until early-fall, I drive wilderness shuttles for Ely Outfitting Company. The work is a great way to collect story ideas and meet fascinating people. The way I see it, when travelers return from an excursion into the Boundary Waters Canoe Area, they've earned bragging rights. They've experienced an adventure many co-workers, family and friends have never had. So when I pick them up, I try to offer a chance to embellish their stories for retelling. These traveling exaggeration seminars aren't in my job description. But I hope they're a fun, final addition to the Duluth pack of memories paddlers bring back from the wilderness.

A couple of simple questions can ignite a firestorm of raucous storytelling inside the shuttle. "What's the first thing you'll tell someone about your trip?"

Some people really get into it and craft some humdingers. The group who conjured the story above did it before we arrived back at the shop. No telling how much more they threw on after they embarked for home.

One retired Marine mapped a self-challenging solo paddle across some wild terrain. For companionship and grit, he bungeed a Chuck Norris action figure to the front seat of his canoe before departing. Shortly into his story after the trip, that rubber doll sprang to life. It spirited the guy up the rockiest, steepest portages and tenderly guided a lost black bear cub back to its mama.

Exaggeration basically means that nothing about reality matters. You can say anything—unless you genuinely want the listener to fall for it. In those cases, don't bloat the plotline. Put a lid on becoming separated from the group, fragility from starvation and teetering on the gunwales of death. Just put more pounds on the fish and more fish on the stringer.

If the story is about a bear entering camp, correct the paddlers who insist it be a grizzly. Compelling as grizzlies might be, northern Minnesota doesn't have any. But maybe a wolf, moose or lynx would suffice better than a bear. Also, ask if they'd prefer drama, humor or cute. One couple encountered a beaver each night who was intent on filching the logs they had put up for the morning fire.

Finally, if quality overrides quantity for a fish tale, swapping out the species is a useful storytelling tool. A 14-inch smallmouth is nice. Changing it to a 14-inch crappie is a slab to behold. But for realism, don't limit-out the harvest. If word gets around, there could be legal consequences.

from *Woods Reader*, spring 2020

Wing Spread

All hell broke loose, webbed feet and wingtips scrambling across the water from the shoreline behind the lilies. The young hooded merganser rocketed out inches over the surface, then gained altitude as she fled the nest. With the feathers of her comb quiffed back, she had the keys to the car and the radio cranked.

She and Del were singing "little runaway" halfway across the lake until she lowered her landing gear, cupped her wings and skidded gracefully to rest. Her adolescent shape bobbed on the light chop. With a quack more like a squawk, her up-tempo numbers careened from greenstone to greenstone at three-second intervals for over an hour.

Unable to sit still for long amid her revelry, she relentlessly practiced takeoffs and landings. Using the same two locations just fifty yards apart, she circled overhead and buzzed the towering cedars. Beneath the water, a turtle at each end of her runway poked their noses through the surface, monitoring intently, her air traffic control.

She questioned going home. With siblings growing as fast as her but devoid of ambition, the nest was getting a little cramped. Out here her head felt so clear. Flight euphoria opened her to guidance, trust and intuition.

Catching her breath, she noticed something she hadn't before. It was either a submerged log or a four-foot fish. If it were a fish, she'd have to tell the family; it'd feed them for a week. It wasn't moving, but it also wasn't there a moment ago. Ah, time enough for thought later. She collected herself to have another go around the lake.

Five feet off the water, a mouthful of razors snapped at her just out of reach. But rather than tarry over escape, she circled back and came in from behind, three feet above the fish. The different angle let her get a glimpse: greenish body, white splotches dashed from head to tail and dullish-red fins.

She did go back home. She told her folks the fish story. The next day, she found where they hid the keys and struck out again.

Resurgent Perspective, Part 2

Dementia and heartbreak began getting a grip on my dad in his later years. Unlike the earlier accounts of his baseball career in "Resurgent Perspective, Part 1," his stories took a turn for the worse. Their reality went beyond playful embellishment. They inflated to some doozies and carried more bleak consequences.

Family members noticed him wearing a ring that none of us had ever seen before. It was a World Series championship ring from 1961. He said he received it as a gift from baseball legend Roger Maris who was his teammate in the minors. Until that story decades later, he had never mentioned Maris.

1961 was also the year Maris hit sixty-one homeruns to break Babe Ruth's single-season homerun record. However, the record is famous for an asterisk as well. Maris had more games in the season than Ruth to hit those homeruns. So an asterisk was placed beside the "61" in record books to indicate the shortcoming. But some baseball historians argue that the asterisk is a slap in the face, as if the achievement doesn't count or didn't even happen.

As mentioned in part one of this story, my dad did have a roommate in the minors who went on to become a well-known major leaguer, Rocky Colavito. Dad told stories about him often and I got to meet him once. Colavito was a coach for Cleveland at the time. When the team came to Chicago to play the White Sox, Dad took me to a game at Comiskey Park. Our tickets were in the nosebleeds. But before the game, he sweet-talked the usher in the box seats to let us stand beside the Cleveland dugout so Dad could introduce me to his former teammate. I got to shake Colavito's hand. He told me to call him Rocky. Plus, his uniform number matched his name in the scorecard, so there was proof that Dad's story was true.

But that's also why my dad's story of Roger Maris' World Series ring didn't add up. If someone of Maris' baseball status was one of Dad's teammates, we sure as hell would have heard about him for years, too, not just Colavito.

What's more, along with the story itself, there were indications that the ring was a fake. In piecing it together, we suspected the ring was purchased from a shyster my dad spent too much time with at a local bar.

Baseball is measured in quantifiable numbers like batting averages, runs scored and pitch-counts. These analytics supposedly translate into winning games. However, they're so dissected and clinical they exclude joyous intangibles of the game. They don't measure heart. They don't offer myth and romance.

Perhaps the most fiercely debated moment in all of baseball history was Babe Ruth's "Called Shot" in the 1932 World Series between the Chicago Cubs and the New York Yankees at Wrigley Field. The only verifiable fact of that moment happened on film during Ruth's at-bat in the fifth inning. He raised his arm and pointed—somewhere. Everything after that is a dispute.

Some say he was pointing to centerfield, "calling his shot" to where he was about to hit the ball. Others claim he was taunting the Cubs' dugout or the fans behind it. Still other interpretations insist that Ruth was pointing at the pitcher; or showing he had two strikes on him; or one strike left; or just one pitch is all it takes to hit the ball.

When that pitch came in, he launched it over the fence into the centerfield seats. Even an ego the size of The Babe's tap danced around the controversial gesture for years. "It's in the papers, isn't it?" he said when first interviewed. "Why don't you read the papers?"

Since then, the Called Shot has been dramatized in books and movies. Actors portraying Ruth theatrically point beyond the centerfield fence. No one will ever know for sure if he legitimately called it. But for over ninety years, the mystery and fantasy of it have delighted millions of fans.

I've asked myself if Babe Ruth really called his shot. I've pondered if that asterisk should appear beside Roger Maris' homerun record. And if it did, should I tag my dad with an asterisk because of how he shaped his stories? Did they happen? Do they matter?

I ask. But I don't answer. The appreciation is in recognizing all of the stories.

For music at my dad's memorial, I wanted to send him around the bases a final time with "Take Me Out to the Ball Game." It wasn't listed in the memorial program and only a handful of us were in on it. As we know from the movie *A League of Their Own*, there's no crying in baseball and I'd been holding my emotions together fairly well until that point in the ceremony. But even though I knew it was coming, I lost it the moment the introductory notes bellowed through the sanctuary.

The whole congregation instantly knew what to do and started singing. The organ was so loud, like I was standing with my ear pressed against an upper deck speaker in a major league ballpark but the volume didn't hurt my ears. It plunked me legless. This was the Church of Baseball.

I only know three things for sure: He was my dad. He taught me baseball. He gave me his time.

Ghosts of a Thought

A turtle the size of a dog bootie laid motionless on the snow-covered trail. Small as it was, it caught the attention of the musher driving her dog team toward the next checkpoint in the race. Soon other turtles like it appeared, dozens of them.

And the musher began to weep.

She was concerned about returning the turtles to water and the safety of their homes. But with temperatures in the forties below zero, every pond and lake was frozen for hundreds of miles.

The musher was Colleen Wallin, a perpetual top-ten finisher in the John Beargrease Sled Dog Marathon. At the time of her turtle episode, the Beargrease showcased nearly four-hundred miles of trail. It ran beside the North Shore of Lake Superior from Duluth, Minnesota, to just south of the Canadian border, and back.

Colleen's strategy for that race included a fast stop at a later checkpoint simply to reload snacks for the team, change booties on some dogs and fill her Nalgene water bottle. Though she stored the bottle in an insulated holder, it somehow didn't slide back properly and the water began to freeze. When she needed it later, she had to muscle off the cover and use a knife to chisel out as much water she could. Then she began seeing turtles.

Colleen's sister Mo was one of her dog handlers. No sooner did Mo hear the turtle stories, than she forced Colleen to chug three consecutive bottles of warm Gatorade. She also insisted that Colleen eat and sleep for a few hours.

Colleen was hallucinating, a condition that occasionally infiltrates musher psyche during marathon-distance events. It's often caused by sleep deprivation, dehydration or both.

Once rehydrated, Colleen was able to reflect, reassemble and retell her adventure: The turtles were actually dog booties that had fallen off the paws of other teams on trail.

Dehydration had monkeyed with her head earlier in her career, too. On that occasion, she was crossing a lake during a ground blizzard and approached a cabin. Its lights glowed from inside like a Terry Redlin painting. Blizzard notwithstanding, she could clearly see her husband Ward and another handler. They were leaning against a beautiful porch railing at the cabin and wearing yellow sunglasses. Colleen was furious. They were *supposed* to be handling dogs for her.

In reality, the cabin was a mirage. In reality, Ward and the handler were at a checkpoint waiting for her arrival. In reality, she wasn't quiet about what she thought she saw and lit into them. Everyone nearby started looking toward their truck.

"Okay you guys!" she barked. "I'm in a ground blizzard on a lake and you two are standing there, just standing there on the porch with your stupid yellow sunglasses, watching and not helping!"

Recognizing the situation, Ward turned to the other handler. "Get some water," he said. "She's dehydrated."

Trail phantasms are familiar territory in the Wallin family and Ward has not been exempt. He said one of his most memorable occurred during his first run of the Can-Am Crown Marathon in Maine. A heavy, wet snow had amassed shortly into the race and compounded the grueling conditions of a two-hundred-fifty-mile trail already designed to be extraordinarily rugged.

Being his first time, Ward didn't know many of the Eastern mushers. But he and his team took up traveling with two French Canadian teams as a group for safety. One, Andre Longchamps, spoke no English. The other, Robert Fredette, spoke some English and became interpreter. Unfortunately, Robert fell behind, leaving Ward and Andre to figure ways to communicate. Ward had been breaking most of the trail and tried to encourage Andre to take a turn, but Andre didn't catch on.

Over time, they joined other mushers including Matt Carstens. Ward asked him to spend some time up front to give his lead dog Lizzie a rest. She'd been in snow up to her neck. In this way, teams leap-frogged each other as they traveled, sharing the grind of being in lead on unbroken trail. Finally, they reached a long, downhill stretch and Ward saw a light on a hill ahead. He asked Matt about it, but only received a baffled look in return. The conversation that followed almost became an argument:

"Is that the checkpoint ahead up on that high hill?" Ward asked. "It looks like the lights of a semi-truck."

"What are you talking about?" Matt replied.

"Is that the checkpoint up there by those lights? I mean we've been at this for hours."

"I don't know what the hell you're looking at, Ward."

"Don't you see those lights? It looks like it's a Peterbilt truck with its headlights shining up on that high hill over there."

"There is no hill over there."

"I thought you said you've run this race before."

"I have."

"Well, there's a hill there. Right there!"

"What are you smoking, man? There's nothing."

Though Ward had consumed all his water, he said he had turned to absolute mush. He was the only one seeing lights. Word of it traveled the trail, too, and other mushers let him know it. "Hey Yankee," one razzed. "Thanks for blazing a great trail. Did the headlights of the semi show the trail for you?"

Ward has run the Can-Am many times since and has made good friends in the process. He prides himself on knowing a trail and its landmarks. But this aberration lingered. When he returned for subsequent races, he still couldn't recollect where that long downhill was. "After maybe the third time, I quit looking around because there was no high ridge where that semi was parked," he said. "It was snowing so damn hard and I was tired and…oh, God."

Shaking the effects of visions can vary. Beargrease veteran Shawn McCarty said he was having a pretty uneventful run three days into the race. He'd had about six hours of sleep since its start. Then from nowhere, he noticed a highway-sized billboard advertising for State Farm Insurance slightly off trail. He pushed on and eventually the billboard disappeared on its own. "It didn't move with me," he said. "It was just there and I went by it."

But common sense kicked in once he realized the State Farm billboard was gone. He said it looked real, then remembered there are no billboards on-trail. However, he questioned its real-world correlation. "I don't have State Farm and I don't think about insurance a lot."

Those later days on the Beargrease trail can take a mental toll and showed no mercy on seasoned musher Peter McClelland. He said his dogs know that running the race includes mandatory rest along the way. So the dogs hunker down and sleep hard immediately when given the chance. They know they'll be on-trail again shortly. But sleep isn't that easy for Peter. He's busy caring for the team and he can't fall asleep on demand. He often just lays down without getting a wink.

During the early-morning hours of the third night, only the small circle of light from his headlamp illuminated the woods. Then gradually, within the timber, Peter began seeing colossal, multicolored fish. They were twenty feet tall and swimming in and out of the trees like in an aquarium. He shook his head and they'd vanish only to reappear later.

Peter had kept tropical fish when he was in high school. But that possible link to real life might sound humdrum compared to a hallucination he'd heard about. It involved a well-known Iditarod musher who saw risqué images. "And boy," Peter wondered, "I see fish."

Veterinarian and musher Jen Freking takes a scientific, matter-of-fact view of hallucinations she's enjoyed throughout her career. She's twice finished second in the Beargrease marathon. The first was her rookie year of the race. But she also experienced one of her favorite hallucinations.

Fatigue had set in by the second night. Moonlight from behind the trees cast linear blue shadows across the darkness as she came upon a straight, flat section of trail. She said that type of terrain is less stimulating, the team gets lulled into a rhythm and the dogs just lope along. It's a setup for drowsiness.

Without warning, a collapsed stepladder materialized in the middle of the trail. Her heartrate skyrocketed, she jolted awake and braced herself for the collision. But as soon as she ran over the ladder, she looked back. The ladder wasn't there.

"It was nothing too serious, just hilarious," she said, "a little hallucination from fatigue…I must have connected those shadows with something that looked like a ladder."

Every marathon musher interprets these close-to-true encounters in their own way. But as a group, mushers are a close and generous community. Mention a hallucination to one musher and they can name the musher it happened to. Their sense of collaboration complements their competitive spirit and radiates a willingness to help shepherd everyone across the finish line. Their stories have taught winter survival, kindled friendships, sparked laughter, and for Colleen Wallin, scored a box of chocolate turtles from co-workers when she returned to everyday life.

About the author

As a freelance writer, Scott Stowell was a regular contributor to the "Outdoor Weekend" section of the *Minneapolis Star Tribune*. His writing, publishing and media background also includes work as a magazine and newspaper editor, radio copywriter, television news field photographer, and high school English and video production teacher. Some of his published pieces have received individual and collaborative awards from the Minnesota Newspaper Association.

Many of the stories in *Back Road Grace* have been broadcast on *Stay Human,* a literary program at public radio station KAXE/KBXE Northern Community Radio in Grand Rapids and Bemidji, Minnesota.

Though born and raised in two very large metropolitan areas, his parents made sure he had substantial exposure to the natural world. As a result, nature and writing became dominant interests in his life and he gravitated northward. He and his wife DyAnne Korda live in Ely, Minnesota, with their Alaskan husky Mustang Sally.